Dear Melina,

Remember there are No Limits...

Wishing you the best on your own leadership Journey!

THE
NAVY
SEAL
ART
OF
WAR

LEADERSHIP LESSONS FROM THE WORLD'S MOST ELITE FIGHTING FORCE

THE
NAVY
SEAL
ART
OF
WAR

ROB ROY
with CHRIS LAWSON

CROWN
BUSINESS

NEW YORK

Published in the United States by Crown Business, an imprint of the Crown Publishing Group, a division of Penguin Random House LLC, New York.
www.crownpublishing.com

CROWN BUSINESS is a trademark and CROWN and the Rising Sun colophon are registered trademarks of Penguin Random House LLC.

Crown Business books are available at special discounts for bulk purchases for sales promotions or corporate use. Special editions, including personalized covers, excerpts of existing books, or books with corporate logos, can be created in large quantities for special needs. For more information, contact Premium Sales at (212) 572-2232 or e-mail specialmarkets@randomhouse.com.

Library of Congress Cataloging-in-Publication Data
Roy, Rob.
The navy SEAL art of war : leadership lessons from the world's most elite fighting force / Rob Roy, Chris Lawson.
pages cm
1. Leadership. 2. Decision making. 3. United States. Navy. SEALs. I. Lawson, Chris. II. Title.
HD57.7.R695 2015
658.4'092—dc23   2014038613

ISBN 978-0-8041-3775-1
EBOOK ISBN 978-0-8041-3776-8

Printed in the United States of America

Book design by Ralph Fowler / rlfdesign
Jacket design by Michael Nagin

10 9 8 7 6 5 4 3 2

First Edition

To my wife, Fia, and our two children, Emille and Adrian
—Rob Roy

To my amazing wife, Jessica, whom I utterly adore. It's been said that
some people live an entire lifetime wondering if they've made a difference to this world.
Just like the SEALs, you don't have that problem. Thank you for saying "Yes."
—Chris Lawson

CONTENTS

CONTENTS

THE
NAVY
SEAL
ART
OF
WAR

NAVAL SPECIAL WARFARE ETHOS/CREED

In times of war or uncertainty there is a special breed of warrior ready to answer our Nation's call. A common man with uncommon desire to succeed. Forged by adversity, he stands alongside America's finest special operations forces to serve his country, the American people, and protect their way of life. I am that man.

My Trident is a symbol of honor and heritage. Bestowed upon me by the heroes that have gone before, it embodies the trust of those I have sworn to protect. By wearing the Trident I accept the responsibility of my chosen profession and way of life. It is a privilege that I must earn every day.

My loyalty to Country and Team is beyond reproach. I humbly serve as a guardian to my fellow Americans always ready to defend those who are unable to defend themselves. I do not advertise the nature of my work, nor seek recognition for my actions. I voluntarily accept the inherent hazards of my profession, placing the welfare and security of others before my own.

I serve with honor on and off the battlefield. The ability to control my emotions and my actions, regardless of circumstance, sets me apart from other men. Uncompromising integrity is my standard. My character and honor are steadfast. My word is my bond.

We expect to lead and be led. In the absence of orders I will take charge, lead my teammates, and accomplish the mission. I lead by example in all situations.

I will never quit. I persevere and thrive on adversity. My Nation expects me to be physically harder and mentally stronger than my enemies. If knocked down, I will get back up, every time. I will draw on every remaining ounce of strength to protect my teammates and to accomplish our mission. I am never out of the fight.

We demand discipline. We expect innovation. The lives of my teammates and the success of our mission depend on me—my technical skill, tactical proficiency, and attention to detail. My training is never complete.

We train for war and fight to win. I stand ready to bring the full spectrum of combat power to bear in order to achieve my mission and the goals established by my country. The execution of my duties will be swift and violent when required yet guided by the very principles that I serve to defend.

Brave men have fought and died building the proud tradition and feared reputation that I am bound to uphold. In the worst of conditions, the legacy of my teammates steadies my resolve and silently guides my every deed. I will not fail.

Waldron in the foreword of author Victor H. Mair's terrific translation of Sun Tzu's text. For Sun Tzu, an enemy's mind and morale is as much an Army's center of gravity as men, technology, and materiel.

That's why I've infused the leadership lessons in this book with the spirit of Sun Tzu. While Sun Tzu offered thirteen chapters, each one devoted to one aspect of warfare, I've spread out my thoughts over fifty-seven chapters. And, of course, I navigate from the battlefield to the boardroom, finding the essential leadership parallels between military and corporate leaders, to make this of use in the corporate world as well as the battlefield.

But like Sun Tzu, my words and experiences stress the importance of evaluation and planning and the need to confront your enemy when he is least prepared. How to best position your forces—both human and material—and manage your financial resources. I underscore the importance of knowing oneself and one's opponent and only going into battle when you have the advantage, to seek out weaknesses in your enemy and to configure your forces in unconventional ways.

Most of all, I embrace Master Sun's wise advice on the need for caring leadership, both on and off the battlefield. You should, too. My favorite quote from *The Art of War*: "Regard your soldiers as your children, and they will follow you into the deepest valleys; look on them as your own beloved sons, and they will stand by you even unto death."

Maxims like these are the backbone of *The Art of War* and so, too, I hope, in *The Navy SEAL Art of War*.

I'd like to think that Master Sun would have made a terrific SEAL. And I know I could have swung a mean Jian in his Army.

AUTHOR'S NOTE

For thousands of years, armies have fought other armies using myriad tactics and strategies to try to win the day. And while Navy SEALs are rightly proud of our warfighting skills, we are also unabashed about taking the lessons learned from history and applying them to our own schemes of battle.

Over my military career, one extraordinary thinker has always stood out: the ancient Chinese general and supreme strategist, Sun Tzu—author of *The Art of War*. Alongside Carl von Clausewitz, Sun Tzu is considered one of the finest military thinkers of all time. And his pithy but powerful work (compared to Clausewitz's more densely delivered *On War*) has inspired me greatly.

What I love about the lessons in *The Art of War* are their simplicity. I've tried to mimic that approach in my own book. Simplicity, according to Adm. William McRaven, a Navy SEAL and former commander of the US Joint Special Operations Command, is what special operators strive for in virtually every operation. In addition to Sun Tzu's simplicity, I love the psychological aspect of his teachings. For Sun Tzu, war is as much about philosophy and psychology as it is about politics and battle. In that manner, he teaches us how to get inside the heads of our adversaries. To "unnerve his opponents, to demoralize them, to mislead them, and to outmaneuver and threaten them, in such a way that their social cohesion breaks down and their rulers and military find themselves in disorder and chaos," to quote Arthur

INTRODUCTION

N O ONE HAD EVER spoken to Paulo like that before. Not his friends, his family, his peers, or his colleagues. Certainly not anyone who worked for him. He's used to being the guy who tells everybody *else* what to do.

But here he was, standing weak-kneed and slump-shouldered on a predawn stretch of San Diego beach. It was 6:47 a.m., or zero 647 as we demonic drivers called it. Our collective voices from the past several hours were still pounding in Paulo's head.

I knew he was at a pivot point.

Paulo's well-tended face was ashen and visibly fallen, sweat sliding down the worn creases of a weathered brow. He was gently rocking from side to side, clearly exhausted and mentally overwhelmed from the physical and mental challenges he'd been facing.

Over the past nine hours, the forty-two-year-old restaurant magnate had been hounded by impatient instructors like me and the increasingly frustrated members of his "boat crew"—his corporate peers—all of them either barking orders or lambasting him for not putting out enough effort or for screwing up some aspect of a training exercise that brought unwanted attention to him or his team. His seven-man boat crew was composed of other successful business executives not unlike himself. They'd all traveled to California to take part in an experience unlike any other in the country: Leadership

Under Fire (LUF), a ninety-hour immersive training course on team building, leadership, and communication run by me and my merry band of macho men. We'd placed "Paulo" on the "Smurf" crew, the team of height-challenged trainees who would sink or swim together over the next three days.

But right here, right now, Paulo was alone—by his own choosing. An instructor for SOT-G—the corporate acronym meaning Special Operations Training Group that I gave my private company—sporting black wraparound cool rays and a blue windbreaker, blue athletic T-shirt, camouflage pants and sand-colored boots, was right up in his grille. So close, in fact, that Paulo couldn't help but smell the coffee on his breath.

Paulo was visibly frustrated. Just moments before, the instructor had plucked him out of the Smurf pack as they suffered another round of "Incentive Physical Training," or IPT, for not properly following simple instructions. Funny how that works with many bosses and leaders—they are good at barking instructions but rarely as good at following them. Even something as simple as counting off feels like advanced trig.

IPT involves endless—and sometimes mindless—push-ups, leg lifts, mountain climbs, you name it. It's meant to emphasize a point, to focus a person's attention on their shortcomings. Unfortunately, Paulo hadn't been giving the required effort. He'd checked out.

More troubling, however, was that it was clear he was close to just saying "screw it" to the whole LUF experience.

"Do you really think that's how you develop loyalty and commitment on a team, by giving up—by letting your teammates down?" asked one of my instructors. "Do you really believe that, sir?"

No response. Paulo just stared blankly out at the pounding surf, saying nothing. He was sweating as if someone had sloshed a bucket of water on his grape, but his lips were clamped tight. He wasn't being belligerent. He simply was not interested. In his head, he'd already quit. Rung the bell. Couldn't take any more. He was in the rationalizing stage and already thinking about next steps.

"Look, you've got to stop thinking about 'what sucks' or 'who's annoying' or whatever it is that you're afraid of," my instructor said firmly. "All you have to do is to focus on what's in front of you at this very moment. Right now. Stop worrying about what's to come, or who hurt your feelings, and start giving one hundred percent to what you're doing *right now*. If you continue freaking yourself out, you'll take yourself completely out of the fight."

Paulo acknowledged the admonishment and slowly shuffled back to join his crew. The Smurfs were told to lock themselves arm in arm and head down to the hard-packed sand at the ocean's edge. Surf torture awaited them all—punishment for being the slowest team at IPT.

"Thanks, Paulo. Great job," one of his teammates muttered. Paulo said nothing.

"Knock that shit off!" shouted another Smurf, a blond buzz-cut fellow who was serving as the team leader. "Let's just do this and move on! One team! Mission first."

But Cool Rays had one more piece of advice for Paulo. "It's not for me or your buddies to motivate you, sir," the gravelly-voiced instructor whispered matter-of-factly in his ear. And then, much louder: "STOP FEELING SORRY FOR YOURSELF!"

Unfortunately for everyone, Paulo called it quits less than an hour later. No amount of encouragement, inspiration, or shame could change his decision. He wanted out and was quickly gone.

"I'm done. It's not for me. Maybe some other time," Paulo told me later. I knew better. His arrogance, and his unwillingness to serve as part of a larger, well-connected team that shared adversity, was held accountable for their actions, and ultimately cared about something bigger than themselves was evident. But he was right. It wasn't for him. And that's too bad. More than anyone else, Paulo needed the sort of training we provide.

Twenty-one others remained, however. And they bloomed where they were planted. And at the graduation ceremonies three long days later, they were never more proud of themselves.

Welcome to Leadership Under Fire, a unique no-holds-barred, no-ego-spared executive training program run by me and my staff of fellow former SEALs.

After 23 years, 11 months, and 23 days in the Navy, 20 of those years as a SEAL, including a stint with the vaunted SEAL Team Six, I decided to conduct "hostile makeovers" of America's business leaders and professionals and, occasionally, reorient and motivate organizations like the football and water polo teams of the University of California, Los Angeles. Leadership Under Fire is where hot-running corporate and professional wunderkinds pay thousands of dollars to shore up their leadership and communication skills at the hands of America's most elite special warfare operators: the US Navy SEALs.

These guys and gals want a change in their lives, and we're here to give it to them. The SEALs are a brand . . . a brand of excellence. We help them understand why that is. We don't try to make SEALs out of them. But we are going to ensure they start thinking—and acting—like SEALs. With excellence.

Before he had decided to leave the program, I watched as Paulo waddled down to the ocean's edge. Along with his boat crew, he soon got down on his knees and rolled over onto his back. He then lay down in the surf zone with his head pointing out to sea. His feet pointed toward the beach and my unforgiving instructors. As ordered, the Smurfs locked arms and waited for the rolling surf of the 57-degree water to brutally wash over their faces and bodies. It wasn't waterboarding. But to Paulo and his team, I know it sure felt like it.

"Get your head and shoulders down in the water!" one of my eagle-eyed instructors bellowed. "You need to be getting wet and sandy."

At this point, I didn't know if Paulo was going to make it or not. Fittingly, I was seated on a two-hundred-pound log with ADVERSITY carved into the side. The students would lift and carry the log later that morning.

The instructor who had berated Paulo a few minutes earlier scampered up to my perch and said that Paulo was thinking about quitting. That he said he didn't think he could take much more of the training.

I'd heard it all before.

"We're going to have to keep a close eye on him, Pops," I said to my instructor. "The little negative voices inside his head are telling him to get the hell out of here. That he doesn't need this."

The trouble was, I lamented, "Paulo needs this training more than anyone here. I hoped he would let us help him grow."

I put on the Leadership Under Fire program a few times each year in conjunction with the Young Presidents' Organization (YPO), a networking and mentoring group that unites more than 21,000 chief executives at leading companies generating more than $6 trillion and employing more than 15 million people in 125 countries. Their shared mission: creating "Better Leaders Through Education and Idea Exchange."

YPO touts "the value of a peer network and trusted mentors, the importance of ongoing education, and the need for a 'safe haven,' where issues can be aired in an environment of confidentiality." It's a powerful network.

Over the past four years, Leadership Under Fire has become one of the most popular seminars the organization sponsors. My company, SOT-G, conducts similar but smaller-scaled training for other companies and organizations throughout the year, but the YPO events are the biggies.

The twenty-three men who signed up for this seminar were finding out why. They were leaders in tech, pharmaceuticals, construction, media, you name it. Their expertise spanned the entire S&P 500 spectrum. What they shared, however, was a quest for excellence and a desire to become the best team leaders they could be.

Most were gleefully drinking from the fire hose. Others, like Paulo, were struggling.

The ninety-hour training began calmly enough at the Loews San Diego hotel at nine o'clock on a Friday night. Hours before, the businessmen and their peers had funneled into the hotel's conference room from all parts of the country. They'd taken limos or taxis to the venue, most hoisting matching luggage and many wearing crisp-pressed casual clothes. Big smiles splashed across most everyone's face as they wandered into the luxury hotel and sipped lemon water from glistening glass dispensers that awaited them. Soon they checked into their lush, lavish rooms. Little did they know they wouldn't return to those rooms for more than seventy-two hours. That my canvas tents and cots would be their only comfort and hot water would be a thing of the past.

I told them all to muster in the hotel conference room by 9 p.m. for their welcome orientation. Awaiting them in the room were not PowerPoint presentations and bottled water but, rather, lean-muscled, steely-eyed former Navy instructors who towered over neat rows of black canvas bags we'd packed and provided. The backpacks contained everything the trainees would need for the next three days. A pair of black swim fins was attached to each bag. The mood was casual if tense. Anticipation was high.

Within minutes, I stepped to the middle of the room and asked everyone to gather around and pipe down. "Welcome," I said. "I want you all to know one important thing before we get started: *I will not let you fail.* I want you to get that into your head right now. *I will not let you fail.* But you have to help me make that happen."

I then spent the next ten minutes preaching my leadership gospel to the assembled.

"First, I want you to stop asking about the schedule. What's next is what's next. Get used to it.

"Right now, what we're looking for from you is effort. It's not about the completion of something. It's the effort. I want you to give one hundred percent, one hundred percent of the time. Do you understand that?"

The wide-eyed trainees nodded their heads in silence, rapturously listening to me. Navy SEALs are used to commanding respect and I exuded the same.

"Some of you are going to get injured. That's to be expected. If you're injured, you're out. No question. That said, many more of you are going to get hurt. That's pride manifesting itself. I don't care about hurt. Neither do my instructors. This training is *supposed* to hurt. We're not going to rub your belly or pat your bottom, or whatever else your mothers did to you to make you feel better when you hurt. We're not going to tell you that you did a great job and that we're proud of you. Get that through your heads right now."

A few sheepish grins and comments bounced around the room. Good-natured shoves from one man to another—a way of saying, "You hear that, bro? He's talking to *you!*"

"Okay," I continued. "Here are some other rules. You need to move with a purpose. We're going to give you clear, concise, and precise direction and we expect you to follow it quickly. There will be times we expect you to lead. There will be times we expect you to follow. We're going to see how you handle things when they get all jacked up. Are you the sort who takes charge and takes care of your people, or are you one of the one-way guys who care only about themselves?"

What I offer these business men and women is not something they are going to get from reading a book. Just like it is in the SEALs, real leadership is a visceral experience. Motivation is not leadership, I remind them. Real leaders inspire, direct, guide, and give hope. That's what I'm all about.

And that's what this book is all about, too. Leadership, SEAL-style. Now let's get cracking. We've got work to do. Don't be a Paulo. Never quit. Ever. Remember, you're never out of the fight.

. . .

THERE'S A GREAT EQUALIZER at the Navy's Basic Underwater Demolition/SEAL school, affectionately known as BUD/S, where the wannabes are separated from the gonnabes. It's known as Log PT. Hoisting an eight-to-ten-foot-long, 300-pound hardwood log (think telephone pole) high over your head as you perform squats, bench presses, and run up and down sand berms for more than two hours is one of the toughest physical evolutions—SEAL-speak for an event—a prospective Navy SEAL has ever done—will ever do—in his life. It certainly was for me. It didn't take long for me to learn that if not for the collective efforts of the six-man "boat crews," life under the log just isn't worth living.

But therein lies the genius of Hell Week, some of the most physically and mentally demanding special operations training our military has to offer: First is the realization that *the only way out is through.* So quit making excuses and get to it. Second, someone out there might be better, faster, and stronger than you. But better, faster, stronger than your SEAL team? Not likely.

Forget the movies. Individual heroes don't last long in my business—or any business for that matter. Even successful SEAL team leaders know their achievement comes as a result of the dynamic, high-performing *teams* they assemble, train, and lead. With preparation and teamwork, SEALs know they can confidently take on any situation or foe this world has to offer.

It's all about the Teams.

Whether it's direct action warfare, special reconnaissance, counterterrorism, or foreign internal defense, SEAL teams are in their element when there's nowhere else to turn—and they've got to get out of it together. As the Navy likes to say, SEALs achieve the impossible "by way of conditioned response, sheer willpower and absolute dedication to their training, their missions *and their fellow spec ops team members.*" I couldn't agree more.

Log PT embodies that belief. Everyone must lift their eighteen inches of the log or else their teammates suffer, forced to make up the difference. At the start, we all have the same lift, the same pressure. But if someone quits or doesn't put out 100 percent, the load quickly gets redistributed down the line. The log doesn't care. It still weighs 300 pounds. Your teammates surely care, however. As SEALs, we're in this together—or we are not.

Those who refuse to dig down deep and push through pain are not the individuals I want on my SEAL team. Thankfully, we have Hell Week for that. We all know the guy who quits something tough and then rationalizes it all day long. Some even try to martyr themselves in the process. "I didn't want to hold my team back," they'll say. Well gee, thanks! Because you quit—or couldn't dig deep enough—the rest of us now have to carry this 300-pound nut buster the rest of the way without you. The mission is still there. Like the log, it doesn't quit.

Those guys piss me off, they really do. *I* know they can make it, but *they* don't know they can make it. Loyalty, dedication, and perseverance are a foreign language to them. They refuse to suck it up and *just lift the fucking log.* They'll quit and whine about it the rest of their lives, instead of living in the now and putting it all on the table. That's why a guy who's going to be a SEAL *knows* he's going to be a SEAL. They just lift the log and push on until their arms explode. And guess what, the rest of us will gladly carry a guy like that the rest of the way, because he's shown that he deserves our devotion. He deserves to be on our team.

IT'S NOT THE COLD, choppy Pacific that puckers them. It's the darkness. It's always the darkness.

Ten times a year, usually around midnight, I clamber aboard one of several civilian-style, rigid rubber raiding craft packed with fifteen to twenty business leaders. Each camouflage-clad client has paid thousands of dollars to participate in a ninety-hour leadership crucible that will test their energy, resolve, and confidence. Most important, it will gauge their ability to lead under fire.

My team and I, composed of active-duty and former Navy SEALs, convey quiet confidence as we motor our charges to our objective, deep in the heart of San Diego Bay. We exude authority with every steely, squinted glance, or hushed commands: "grab hold of something," "check your gear," or "shut the hole under your nose." It's dramatic—that's intentional—and the tension grows with every whitecap the boat crosses. At a predetermined time and place, unbeknownst to our well-paying passengers, we abruptly splash them out of the boats and into the coal-black water. The sky around and overhead is equally inky, the only illumination coming from the drumstick-thick green or yellow chemlights tied to their flotation devices. Surrounded by fellow strangers in the wide-open ocean— and immediately harangued by me and my team—these industry hotshots soon start swimming for their very lives—even though they have no idea where they are going or what they've gotten into. The one-wayers quickly sprint for the shore, never looking back, uberconfident in their individual "aren't I impressive" abilities. Those left in their wake begin fending for themselves. Some bob slowly, aimlessly in circles, fear and indecision evident in their eyes. Still others, without prompting from me, rally their compadres with words of inspiration, guidance, and hope. They lead by example, unsure of what to do and yet decisive, bringing people together in a one-for-all push to the safety of the surf zone. Two miles later, as everyone lies exhausted and splay-legged on the beach (and I've applauded them on their physical accomplishment), the first of many leadership evaluations is held. We don't pull punches. Who froze up and didn't make the right calls?

Who showed proper situational awareness? Who was the guy or gal that others looked to for strength and inspiration? Who undermined others to get a better position? Who built bonds with those around them? Who can tell me if every person who went in the water with them made it safely ashore? Who acted like a Navy SEAL would act?

Leadership Under Fire is built on the very principles that Navy SEALs use to build dynamic, successful, high-performance teams out of alpha-dog individuals. Since 2005, SOT-G has teamed with the YPO to help further develop the leadership abilities of its members. SOT-G helps the YPOers become more successful executives through a challenge only we can provide. We help them learn to build teams that thrive on change and adversity, embody resilience, and grow despite today's marketplace challenges. The same sorts of teams every business needs today—the same teams *your* business needs today.

As members of the most elite Special Operations community in the world, my team and I have designed this unique program around what works. I've been called "America's toughest CEO coach." My mission is to conduct hostile makeovers of corporate clients, making them better, tougher, smarter bosses. Our clients are immersed in the warriors' mindset, coupled with the leadership and team-building concepts of the US Navy SEALs. Because *we train the way we fight*: there is no second place, there are no do-overs, there are no excuses. We emphasize unique physical challenges in order to expose a person's mental and emotional attitudes and capabilities. Only then can we truly evaluate their strengths or weaknesses using a simulated combat environment.

We believe the course is a rare opportunity to analyze the foundations of leaders. We offer an experience where powerful leadership and effective teamwork are more than just concepts—they're necessities. When they graduate, clients take home tools and experiences that are impossible to replicate outside the Special Operations community.

Those tools and experiences can prove crucial in today's business environment, where increased focus is being placed on fully utilizing and leveraging the value of every employee. Strong teamwork and leadership can help increase productivity, reduce turnover, and boost morale. In this book, I take the most effective training exercises and SEAL team principles I've learned over the years—the ones that have shown they work across widely different disciplines—and offer them as tools that any manager, executive, or individual can use in life and in their career. And it's all built on the best practices and experiences of U.S Navy SEALs. We teach people how to:

- Ensure a two-way flow of communication.

- Build flexible, dynamic organizational structures.

- Acquire and keep important team members.

- Gain the trust and loyalty of team members.

- Prevent bureaucratic inertia.

- Effectively train their eventual replacements and grow from within.

- Plan and prepare for crises.

- Train others.

- Make better decisions under stress.

- Communicate objectives simply, forcefully, and effectively.

In this book, we will teach you how to:

1. MAXIMIZE performance, increase productivity, and enhance efficiency in every aspect of your business and personal life.

2. MAKE sound decisions under pressure, lead in any environment, and develop the management skills needed to unlock your own full potential, and that of your organization.

3. DEVELOP greater resilience and flexibility in the face of intense pressure.

4. STRENGTHEN your mental fortitude and physical ability in order to expand what you are capable of doing and improve productivity.

5. DEVELOP the tools needed to support maximum performance, and eliminate habits or preexisting beliefs that compromise the success of your objectives.

6. TAP into a deep reservoir of energy and purpose, leveraging your fears into creating opportunities that did not previously exist.

7. ENHANCE your ability to win, whatever the situation or environment.

The Navy SEAL Art of War gathers together fifty-seven of the SEAL maxims I've learned, developed, and taught over my years as both a SEAL leader and a coach to business executives. While these maxims cover a wide range of military-themed subjects—from high-altitude jumps, sniper training, and close-quarters combat to boarding and capturing an enemy vessel—they are easily applied to many aspects of one's life and work. They are sometimes unconventional, but they are effective, necessary, and battle tested. I believe the maxims are the tools that readers will take with them as they face and overcome life's challenges. This is not a long book, but I think you'll find it chock-full of insights and useful advice. It can be read straight through, or bookmarked with the principles you want to reference later, when facing opposition or opportunity.

. . .

I NEVER WANTED TO BE a pipe-swinging frogman. But then, isn't that how destiny so often works?

My Special Forces adventure began in 1983, when, on a lark, I applied to become a Navy SEAL. I did it at the behest of some of my fellow gym rat friends, who thought my small, muscled, five-foot-eight, 225-pound frame could use a new challenge. At the time, I was a twenty-two-year-old sailor, an aircraft avionics technician by training, assigned to the US Navy station in Rota, Spain. When I wasn't working on F-14 Tomcats, EA-6B Prowlers, or F/A-18 Hornets, I was playing fullback for the command football team, or benching my body weight in the fitness center. I was a happy jock, but I was more than ready to trade my Spanish sabbatical for a new opportunity.

I honestly had no idea what the SEALs were, let alone what they actually did or how they trained. Remember, these were pre-YouTube days and I was stuck out in the middle of the Mediterranean. One of my friends said he'd heard that SEALs were essentially Navy poster boys: guys who worked out all day and flacked for the Navy. It sounded like a terrific fit for me. Before I knew it, I was off to Coronado, California, home of SEAL Beach and the headquarters of Naval Special Warfare. I quickly learned the meaning of the phrase "Welcome to the Suck."

That impulsive decision turned into a tumultuous, life-changing, twenty-two-year affair with America's most elite Special Operations fighting force—the US Navy SEALs. Since then, like the infamous World War II Marine Raiders, I've carried machine guns like pistols, and knives that were tempered in hell. I've jumped out of perfectly good airplanes and helicopters; dived from nuclear-powered ballistic missile submarines submerged below the ocean surface; and shot just about every weapon with a trigger. I've been part of a team that has invaded foreign countries, killed bad guys, protected ambassadors, and hunted poachers. I've served or trained in jungles, deserts, snow-covered mountains, and every patch of sea, land, or air in between. I've been to war and I've helped stop others.

It's been a helluva ride.

For much of my SEAL career, I served in the elite SEAL Team Six—now known as United States Naval Special Warfare Development Group (DEVGRU)—the same secretive counterterrorism and special mission SEAL team sent in to kill Osama bin Laden in Pakistan in 2011. Being selected for that duty was a miracle in and of itself. DEVGRU was where the best of the best were sent, just as SEAL Team Six remains today. It took a lot of hard work and leadership to get there.

As a result, I've graduated from some of the military's toughest and most highly specialized schools, including Basic Underwater Demolition SEAL school (BUD/S); Naval Special Warfare (NSW) Scout/Sniper School; NSW Winter Warfare Course; NSW Jungle Environment Survival Training; Driving, Shooting, Surveillance, and Counter-Surveillance School; US Army Airborne School; and the US Army Parachute Rigger School, to name a few. I'm an Open Water Dive Master and a Static Line/Freefall Parachuting Jumpmaster.

I've also served with, trained, or advised fellow Special Operations units around the world, including US Army Special Forces teams, US Air Force Pararescue team, the British SBS, Australia's SAS, Israel Defense Forces, US State Department, Central Intelligence Agency, Illinois State Police, US Customs in Miami, Tampa SWAT team, Los Angeles SWAT team, and forces from Norway, Sweden, Denmark, and Thailand. In recognition of my leadership abilities, I was assigned as a leading chief petty officer for the NSW Motivators—a mentoring group for active-duty Navy SEALs.

In short, as the ballad goes, "I've been around the world twice, and talked to everyone once. I'm a lover, a fighter, an American UDT

SEAL diver. That's a rootin', tootin', shootin,' paratroopin' SCUBA diving, demolition double-cap crippin' frogman—the last of the bare-knuckle fighters.'"

But there's more to the Navy SEAL experience than just the lore. Along the way, I've become—like all my SEAL brothers—a leader of men, a trusted and reliable team member, and an expert in strategy and tactics. I'm someone who thrives in ever-changing, asymmetric situations. The crucible of SEAL training and operations required it. I was blessed to spend the better part of two decades dissecting and internalizing the essential principles of SEAL warfare: how to *shoot, move,* and *communicate* effectively as a *team.* Only by mastering teamwork can our missions be assured of success. The techniques that SEAL teams use to bring people together—shaping dynamic individuals into high-performing teams—is an art, really. An art of war, to be more precise.

And now I'd like to share those secrets and passions with you. I know they can help make you a better boss and a more successful person.

Since 2005, the year I left the SEALs to begin my entrepreneurial adventure as president of SOT-G Corporation, I've trained thousands of corporate, professional, and organizational clients in the art of SEAL leadership. As a result, SOT-G has become one of the world's leading companies specializing in military consultation and leadership training. We train and advise clients how to safely operate in challenging territories around the globe, and work to develop corporate leadership potential to staggering new heights. We focus on leadership and team building, personal growth, risk management, and Special Operations training. We don't teach people how to be SEALs but, rather, how to think and act like them. Trust me, that's more than enough to set you apart from your competition.

In addition to my corporate clients, SOT-G provides real-world

training to the US Navy Visit, Board, Search, and Seizure teams—
the sailors who board and inspect suspicious vessels on the high
seas. Even though I'm out of uniform, I'm still leading sailors on the
deckplates.

I've been able to leverage my special skills, personality, and
training—and those of my SOT-G team—in uniquely entrepreneurial ways. I've become one of the most recognized Navy SEALs in the
world. I've been featured in television reality shows, such as Spike TV's
The Deadliest Warrior and the History Channel's *Mail Call*. I've served
as military advisor to the Hollywood movie blockbuster *Transformers*
and acted in such Hollywood hits as Vin Diesel's *xXx*. I've been the
face of countless US Navy SEAL recruiting campaigns, and was the inspiration and spokesman for Sony PlayStation's SOCOM Navy SEALs
game franchise, where I helped to develop characters, was involved in
creative development, and secured vital military assets for production.

The reason I've been so successful is that my team and I have used
our leadership knowledge and experience to help students, professionals, and business men and women understand what matters
most: their teams, that unique collection of individuals who, when
properly trained, motivated, and led, can achieve astonishing things.

I've watched good, well-intentioned guys and gals become great
leaders—inspiring, guiding, and giving hope to struggling businesses
and individuals—while leading by example and leading from the
front. I've watched competent men and women reach new heights as
leaders, communicators, and team players, as they learned to trust
themselves and one another, tapping into their full potential and
emerging from challenging situations unfazed. Leveraging the same
leadership and teamwork principles that helped Navy SEALs cap-
ture and kill Osama bin Laden, I've helped people just like you learn
to thrive on chaos, knowing exactly what to do when everyone else
around you remains slack-jawed, dazed, and confused.

. . .

THE SEAL ETHOS is timeless and time tested.

It was President John F. Kennedy, a Navy veteran of World War II, who in 1962 called for a small, elite maritime military force to conduct what became known as "unconventional warfare." Navy leadership quickly began to establish guerrilla and counterguerrilla units, with a nod to the Army Green Berets. The SEALs were born to carry out the types of "clandestine, small-unit, high-impact missions that larger forces with high-profile platforms (such as ships, tanks, jets and submarines) cannot," as the Navy puts it. In essence, we go where others cannot to carry out the nation's business. If we can't get it done by ourselves—which is rare—we conduct the essential on-the-ground special reconnaissance of critical targets for strikes by larger conventional forces.

We primarily come from the sea but, as our name states, we're able to rain down from the air or infiltrate by land—whatever the mission requires. Like successful businesses, we adapt and improvise. When you consider that half the world's infrastructure and population is located within one mile of an ocean or river, you can see the value of an elite maritime unit.

Today, all around the globe, SEALs are pursuing high-value targets who seek to do our nation harm. We've been very fortunate in that effort in recent years. Along the way, we've learned from past mistakes and continued to hone and develop our craft. But, in the end, the bedrock of that craft always comes down to effective leadership and teamwork.

In the chapters and pages that follow, I'm honored to be your swim buddy and SEAL mentor. All I ask is that you don't give up on me, or yourself. Much of what we'll cover will be way outside your normal wheelhouse. At times, words like *discipline, respect, courage,* and *commitment* might sound like clichés. I assure you that to SEALs—

the folks so many admire when you hear that we just took out three Somali pirates and freed an American ship captain—those words are anything but clichés. They serve as the capital that funds our operational success. I'll help you understand why.

The Navy SEAL Art of War gives you a fresh look at the training of the Navy SEALs. You'll gain a better understanding of the challenges faced by these warriors, and the tools we use to maintain unit cohesion and trust. More important, this book will show you how to apply those same principles in order to improve your own life and career. I'll help you redefine who you are as a leader and show you how to take that improved knowledge to successfully lead your own teams.

Many of you will recognize the parallels between what I'm writing about and the Chinese military classic *The Art of War*, by General Sun Tzu. For more than two thousand years, *The Art of War* has served as mandatory reading for military and business leaders interested in survival and success. Its thirteen chapters provide timeless wisdom on military tactics and strategy. *The Art of War* is a primer on how to thrive and survive on *any* battlefield. As Master Sun said, "Ultimate excellence lies not in winning every battle but in defeating the enemy without ever fighting." That sort of advice applies to much more than the conduct of war, notes Sun Tzu biographer John Minford. "It is an ancient book of proverbial wisdom, a book of life." In the same way, it is my hope that *The Navy SEAL Art of War* will stand proudly alongside the works of other classic military theorists and philosophers, such as Carl von Clausewitz ("War is the continuation of *Politik* by other means"); Marcus Aurelius ("The first rule is to keep an untroubled spirit. The second is to look things in the face and know them for what they are"); and even the Bhagavad Gita ("One who has control over the mind is tranquil in heat and cold, in pleasure and pain, and in honor and dishonor; and is ever steadfast with the Supreme Self").

Two thousand years ago, wars were about generals moving large armies over continents in advance of massive battles involving tens of thousands—or even hundreds of thousands—of men. Today, it's more about asymmetrical warfare, transformational technologies, precision-guided munitions, and counterterrorism techniques. It's about smaller tactical units that can be deployed anywhere in the world within hours, ready for anything. And in the not so distant past, businesses were about huge corporations like General Motors, AT&T, and IBM carving out massive territory across varied fronts as armies did in the time of Sun Tzu. Now it's about nimble and fast-growing companies like Instagram, Pinterest, Apple, and Facebook; it is about entrepreneurs, small business owners, and more established companies making sure their teams react with lightning speed to the changes they encounter every day. More than ever, people in the workplace wake up finding everything they believed about their business and their industry has shifted or disappeared.

Time, like armies, marches on. New ideas and technologies, as well as innovative methods to deploy them, are created daily. With this book, I'd like to offer a new take on the old classic *The Art of War*. Like the original, I hope you'll find it a pithy resource for life and success.

The Navy SEAL Art of War shares the modern-day maxims that make the Navy SEALs America's go-to force when the balloon goes up. I'll teach you concepts like how to develop the Warrior Mindset, how to Evaluate, Plan, Execute, and why you must Deploy the Strong and Develop the Weak; as well as the Art of Deception, the OODA Loop, and why the only easy day was yesterday. And of course I'll bring my own irreverent attitude and personal experiences to illustrate my points.

Navy SEALs protect and serve. But it is American business that creates, delivers, and provides the economic backbone of our country. If you and your colleagues fail, America fails. I'm proud to help you become a better leader, so you can continue to help fuel our powerful economy and our collective quality of life. If I can make your life and career a little richer by sharing what I've learned, I'm excited. But remember, the very first step is recognizing and harnessing your own potential. For some of you, that might require that you rewind the clock—to recall the passion and the desire that got you where you are today. I'll help you get there.

Master Sun said, "If you know the enemy and know yourself you need not fear the results of a hundred battles." *The Navy SEAL Art of War* will teach you *how* to know yourself and know that enemy. More important, it will teach you how to build a dynamic team that will take you over the horizon.

BE READY FOR
WHATEVER THE
BOOGER EATERS
THROW YOUR WAY

N O PLAN SURVIVES first contact with the enemy. That maxim is especially true in what SEALs call *close quarters battle*, or CQB, where homes, hallways, alleys, and streets become war zones in the blink of an eye. For a CQB mission to be successful—like the 2011 bin Laden raid in Abbottabad, Pakistan—extensive planning and training are essential. Nowhere is a SEAL's value as a living, breathing precision-guided munition more necessary. And when it goes right, whether planned or freelanced in real time on site, CQB is an amazing—almost Zen-like—experience to behold: armed frogmen flowing like water through a house or building, shooting, moving, and communicating in an exhilarating, effortless dance of death.

Also known as *close quarters defense* or *close quarters combat*, CQB is one of the most difficult things a SEAL does. Something as intense as hand-to-hand fighting requires that an individual be honed to a razor's edge so that actions aren't debated or deliberated over, but are performed without hesitation. While meticulous planning is essential, successful missions like CQB always circle back to training. When you are well trained everything becomes instinctual. That's the game changer. On a certain level, it's no different than what a football or baseball player or emergency room doctor experiences during critical moments. Repetition (training) leads to memorization and memorization leads to instinct. Therefore, one must train and train their skills until they know a procedure cold. And then they must train some more. In unpredictable situations like combat, such training is the key to victory. That's why the SEALS who got bin Laden didn't bail when one of their stealth helicopters—a modified UH-60 Black Hawk—clipped a compound wall and had to make a hard landing. They had trained for just that kind of scenario. No panic. No problem. Instinct kicked in. They know what to do. Mission on.

It's the same in business. Martin, a CEO of a small printing and graphics company in Maryland, created a culture of endless training for his sales and marketing force after listening to one of my lectures. He says the impact on his team has been miraculous.

"Just when we think we're ready, we now train just a little bit more," he wrote to me. "When it's time to make a presentation to a potential client, a customer, or a board, we don't believe there's any such thing as being over prepared."

As his teams put together their presentations, Martin said, he always asks them: "Are we adding real value? Are we challenging the customer and ourselves? Have we properly learned about the actual people we are planning for?"

"We never just 'wing it,'" he wrote. "There's a real difference in being confident and being cocky. Confident recognizes that there's always something more we can add to the presentation that's unique or specific or counterintuitive for the client. Cocky says 'been there, done that. Let's just do it again.' The SEALs have taught me the value of training—of doing my homework. The customer always knows if you're good, or just mailing it in."

Such rigorous preparation enables Martin's teams to freelance with ease and confidence when necessary. They know how to blow away the client—not bullshit them.

When you have trained to perform on an instinctual level, you can act instead of react. In combat, ironically, bad stuff usually happens because of a *lack* of action. The moment you pause or second-guess, the bad guy may grab a hostage and change the whole equation.

So how does one train for these sorts of successes? By using the crawl, walk, run approach. In SEAL training, first we teach a SEAL to shoot. Then teach him to shoot and run. Then teach him to shoot accurately while running. Then we teach him to do it in total darkness. And so on. Once an individual is proficient, we begin training that skill in myriad conditions, situations, and scenarios—likely gaining real-world experience along the way. Equally as important: we train the way we fight, not the other way around. There's a difference. If one fights the way they train, then they will act like they do on the rifle range. They will pick their weapon up, check it, and do all the safety bullshit, etc. The real world is dirty, aggressive, and intimidating, and one must train that way, too.

COMMANDER'S INTENT

WHEN A MILITARY ACTION absolutely, positively has to be mounted overnight, the president phones 1-800-USN-SEAL. That conversation—as it should be for senior leaders—is always quick and pointed. The commander in chief explicitly states the end goal— "Sink this boat; take out that bad guy; free those hostages," etc.—and rightly leaves the details on how to accomplish that mission to his capable subordinates. No need for micromanagement. The SEALs accept the responsibility and are held accountable for their subsequent actions. More important, they know what needs to be done and what outcome determines and defines the mission's success. *They've been unleashed.*

This vital communication is known in military parlance as "Commander's Intent." Not to be confused with organizational "vision" or "values," Commander's Intent is a clearly defined and articulated goal for a particular mission. Successful leaders—regardless of their operational environment—routinely issue it. By doing so, teams can properly plan and ultimately succeed on the battlefield. Remember, in the fog of war, plans change and confusion reigns. Armed with Commander's Intent, however, dynamic operators on the pointy end of the spear can always press the fight. When everyone clearly knows what right looks like, individuals and small teams are free to deploy their knowledge and creativity when plans go awry. They maneuver in new and asymmetrical ways, develop tactics, techniques, and procedures on the fly, slashing and jabbing through the fog of confusion. No one stands around with their hands in their pockets wondering what to do next. Commander's Intent is, therefore, an empowering tool—a leader's guiding principle—that allows subordinates to display personal initiative in times of uncertainty. In many cases, individual improvisation will be what saves the day—not the original plan.

Imagine a combat scenario where enemy forces are harassing a military convoy route through a specific mountain pass. The commander issues his intent to the operating forces, ordering them to ensure safe passage through the treacherous pass. He does not, however, specify what weapons to use, which routes to take, or what units to send. He simply articulates his intent to clear the route. The details on how to accomplish that are left to subordinate commanders and their charges. To quote General George S. Patton, who could easily have been a SEAL: "Never tell people how to do things. Tell them what to do, and they will surprise you with their ingenuity."

Jonathon is a senior vice president of one of North America's largest building materials manufacturing companies. He's also a recovering micromanager. After years of mowing through talented subordinates who ultimately tired of his overbearing, intrusive leadership style and palpable lack of trust, and quit to take their talent elsewhere, Jonathon attended one of my Leadership Under Fire seminars. He saw how SEALs thrive on a culture of trust. He grudgingly—but laudably—discovered that while successful in his business, he could achieve even greater success if he simply held his supervisors and employees accountable to their assigned tasks and got the hell out of their way. Employee morale—not to mention his own—increased, too. To get there, Jonathon had to learn to curb his obsessive-compulsive, controlling appetite. To his great credit, he even began creating a culture where people actually sought accountability, and acted as if they were part owners of the business.

"Too often I felt that if I didn't hover over a manager, then *my* butt might ultimately be on the line," he told me. "It was tough to let go. But I realized that we actually achieved better results when I gave people the freedom to do the job I hired them to do! That doesn't mean I'm not enthusiastically involved. I am. It's just that I'm no longer *overly involved*."

According to *Entrepreneur* magazine, 90 percent of employees in the organizations included in their "2010 Great Place to Work Rankings: Best Small & Medium Workplaces" report believe management trusts them without looking over their shoulder. Ninety-two percent say they are given a lot of responsibility. How does management achieve this? By doing these five things:

1. Commit to hiring the right people.

2. Make people accountable to one another.

3. Clearly and frequently articulate expectations.

4. Give employees decision-making power.

5. Give employees an ownership stake.

SEALs know that the unbending bedrock of these concepts is trust. To confidently convey intent without micromanaging it, a leader must implicitly trust that his followers are properly manned, planned, and equipped to handle the mission. If one has trained his team properly, however, such trust should be easily bestowed. The best part: receiving such unquestioned trust from a commander will inspire and motivate subordinates in incalculable ways.

Remember the words of David Ogilvy, the father of advertising, who famously said, "Hire people who are better than you are, then leave them to get on with it."

FESTINA LENTE:
MAKE HASTE SLOWLY

WHILE IT MIGHT SOUND counterintuitive, combat leadership and performance is an elegant art. Violent and cutthroat as their craft may be, Navy SEALs exhibit the same elegance we admire in a professional dancer or athlete.

In 2010 I starred in a Spike network reality show called *The Deadliest Warrior.* You may have seen similar shows on other networks where teams of elite commandos duke it out in a series of challenges to determine who the deadliest warrior and protector is.

The Spike show had some interesting hooks, in addition to the traditional mano-a-mano matchups of these reality shows. The producers and hosts showcased twenty-first-century science and the latest in computer-generated image technologies to record quantifiable, evidence-based statistical conclusions. Everything we touched had a sensor attached to it. Every move we made was measured and captured. The result: with withering accuracy—and in high-definition, slow-motion photography—the host and scientists could show viewers whose hands punched harder, knives slashed deeper, which weapons and shooters engaged targets faster and more accurately, or whose explosives delivered more killing power per square inch.

On the episode I was featured in, I was paired with former Navy

SEAL (and demolitions expert) Colin Palmer; we faced off against two former Israel Defense Forces commandos. The competition featured, among other things, knife fights against ballistic dummies (gel-torso mannequins with realistic-looking organs, skeletons, and blood) and combat target shooting using a pig carcass tied to a moving robot. It was, literally, a bloody hoot.

At the end of two days and four intense competitions (using knives, pistols, machine guns, and explosives), the producers uploaded their results and ran a high-tech battle simulation, which they later used to create a scripted, seven-minute battle scene with actors. After 1,000 simulations, the SEALs recorded 518 kills compared to the Israelis' 482. It was close competition, but the SEALs were deemed the Deadliest Warriors.

But what I wanted to point out was that elegance, crazy as it sounds, played a large part in our victory.

While SEALs are usually faster, smarter, and more adaptable than their adversaries, we're also more elegant in how we operate. That elegance translates into lethal accuracy when it matters most.

In my world, elegance is not defined by grace and beauty, style and sophistication. In fact, if you watch the YouTube video of me attacking the gel-torso dummy with my Recon-1 combat knife, you'll see why few folks would describe it as elegant. No, what I'm talking about is a mindset that manifests itself in beautifully tactical action.

Elite combat operators are decidedly elegant individuals. They rely on simplicity, refinement, dignity, inventiveness, and ingenuity. This may reveal itself as poise and performance under fire. Or it might result in an elegantly neat and clever idea or solution. To those practiced in the art of warfare and self-defense, the polished splendor of these elegant actions is both breathtaking and effective.

But you can train yourself to be the same way in the environment you work and perform in.

Think about your favorite quarterback as he drops back to pass under relentless pressure from a thundering phalanx of three-hundred-pound linemen bent on rearranging his spine. The elegant quarterback seems to effortlessly avoid danger, eluding his tacklers and nimbly finding a way to release the ball in a smooth and accurate fashion to his open receivers. He appears calm, methodical, and commanding under pressure. It is clear his mind is focused, and his actions are practiced and measured.

Now imagine yourself in a tremendously stressful, pressure-packed scenario—a production crisis at work, an injured child screaming for help, the potential loss of a huge contract.

Are you the sort who panics, and screams at the top of your lungs or runs around waving your arms like a madman? Do you panic or look to others for help? Do you freeze in fear, losing any chance at gaining a tactical or opportunistic advantage? Do you cave and capitulate?

Or are you the sort who can keep a clear head, and compartmentalize your responses in chaotic situations? Can you emulate the cool and collected quarterback, delivering the required results based on the right decisions? In short, can you perform under pressure with grace, dignity, and selfless command?

The ability to perform under pressure is a SEAL trademark. In fact, it is a requirement. When I went toe-to-toe on the TV show with IDF vet Mike Kanarek, a weapons and tactical knife-fighting expert who also holds more black belts in more martial arts than I could even begin to count, the pressure was intense.

In one contest in particular, I needed to send 30 rounds into a moving target—a pig carcass tied to a maneuvering, tactical robot—at a distance of 75 feet, scoring as many kill shots as I could without harming dozens of innocent, nearby civilians. My weapon of choice: the M4 Colt Commando, a compact 5.56-caliber submachine gun with an 11.5-inch barrel and a rate of fire of 750 to 900 rounds per minute.

As soon as show host Geoffrey Desmoulin yelled "Deploy TacBot!"

I calmly raised the rifle butt to my shoulder, put my cheek on the stock, lined up the M4's iron sights, and began managing my breathing. Within nanoseconds, I started squeezing off well-aimed shots while adapting to the continually shifting scene before me. I made no unnecessary movements, no forced or unwanted actions, gave in to no sense of panic. I tried to remain a model of smooth, artful elegance.

And my score reflected my actions: I fired 30 shots in 34 seconds, and recorded 30 kills, before the target disappeared. I riddled the moving target—the pig—with blistering accuracy. My shot group was tight—all in the neck area—and the exit wounds were devastating. Just as important, no innocent bystanders were harmed, despite the fact that the "terrorist" pig often tried to hide behind them. My opponent, on the other hand, took an achingly long 48 seconds to hit the target just 21 times with his 5.56-caliber Micro Galil, and two of those were grazing shots. Still, he performed well, if slowly, and finished as the first loser.

The key in these cases—as in any stressful situation life throws at you—is to slow down and take the time you need to perform skillfully and with purpose. To be elegant.

I'm often reminded of the Latin adage *Festina lente*. Roughly translated, it means "Make haste slowly," or "More haste, less speed." The Roman emperor Augustus used the motto extensively. Historians tell us Augustus "thought nothing less becoming in a well-trained leader than haste and rashness."

It makes great sense. Why be fast, when accuracy matters more? You must be fast, but only fast enough to be effective.

The best combat shooters follow a like-minded motto: "Slow is smooth, and smooth is fast." It's all about elegance. You want to be smooth, elegant, and as fast as you can be, but within measured reason. Accuracy will always be more important than speed.

So make haste slowly. And carry yourself with elegance.

FRONT SIGHT FOCUS

A S THE ENTIRE WORLD knows now, thanks to the acclaimed movie with Tom Hanks, in 2009, on Easter Sunday, three Navy SEAL snipers rescued an American cargo ship captain and killed three Somali pirates in an amazing display of marksmanship and mission focus. Three single shots. Three quick kills. The *Maersk Alabama* captain was retrieved unharmed, ending a five-day standoff between the US Navy and the band of rogue pirates.

Perched on the fantail of the destroyer USS *Bainbridge* (DDG-96)—after stealthily parachuting into the open Indian Ocean from the belly of an American transport plane just days before—the SEALs readied their rifles equipped with night vision scopes and bipods. Their targets were crammed into an eighteen-foot covered lifeboat being towed less than seventy-five feet away. At dusk, as both the 509-foot *Arleigh Burke*–class guided missile destroyer and the tiny lifeboat bobbed up and down on the roughening seas, ongoing hostage negotiations quickly deteriorated. According to the *New York Times,* the pirates became increasingly agitated and aggressive, after spending more than ninety-six hours in the suffocating lifeboat. At one point, the SEALs reported seeing one pirate menacingly point his AK-47 assault rifle at the tied-up, fifty-three-year-old captain, Richard Phillips. His life, they believed, was in imminent danger. At that moment, the SEALs were given permission to engage. Soon, in a patient, choreographed display of simultaneous precision, all three SEALs acquired their targets. When two of the captors stuck their heads out of a rear hatch for a breath of fresh air, and the third presented himself behind a window in the bow, three well-aimed shots were loosed in amazing synchronization—one from each shooter. The result: three pirates dropped dead to the deck. Mission accomplished.

The attention to detail that's required to pull off such a feat from liftoff to landing requires what we call Front Sight Focus. In civilian circles, it's called keeping your eye on the ball—being laser focused on the mission at hand—despite any distractions that cloud the venue. When you are dialed in properly, no amount of confusion or surrounding chaos should rattle you. Emotions are held in check. Slow becomes fast. You know what needs to be done and focus squarely on seeing to it. You stay in the zone. During training, we toss every conceivable obstacle into the scenario—and turn that upside down the next time out—to force our team to focus relentlessly on the objective. In the *Maersk Alabama* rescue, the pitching decks of both vessels did not deter the sniper's shot placement—troublesome as it was. Neither did the continual shifting positions of their targets, or the previous day's high-altitude, low-opening parachute jump into the open ocean. Such things were merely challenges to overcome, not factors that overwhelmed. By keeping a steely-eyed focus on the front sight, your path is cleared.

To be a good shooter you must have what's known as proper sight alignment and sight picture. You attain that by focusing your eye on the front sight post at the end of the barrel, and centering the top of that post in the rifle's rear sight aperture. You then align those sights at six o'clock on the bull's-eye, paying sole attention to the front sight post. If that focus never wavers—even as the primary target becomes slightly blurry, or the explosive sounds of the battlefield fill the air—a well-aimed shot will always hit the target. It's a powerful metaphor for success in any endeavor.

Daniel Goleman, a codirector of the Consortium for Research on Emotional Intelligence in Organizations at Rutgers University, is an expert on the subject of focus in business. He is the author of *Focus: The Hidden Driver of Excellence*. In an article in the *Harvard Business Review*, Goleman suggests a troika approach to focus the workplace.

"A primary task of leadership is to direct attention. To do so, leaders must learn to focus their own attention," Goleman writes. "When we speak about being focused, we commonly mean thinking about one thing while filtering out distractions. But a wealth of recent research in neuroscience shows that we focus in many ways, for different purposes, drawing on different neural pathways—some of which work in concert, while others tend to stand in opposition.

"Grouping these modes of attention into three broad buckets—focusing on *yourself*, focusing on *others*, and focusing on *the wider world*—sheds new light on the practice of many essential leadership skills," Goleman contends. "Focusing inward and focusing constructively on others helps leaders cultivate the primary elements of emotional intelligence. A fuller understanding of how they focus on the wider world can improve their ability to devise strategy, innovate, and manage organizations.

"Every leader needs to cultivate this triad of awareness, in abundance and in the proper balance, because a failure to focus inward leaves you rudderless, a failure to focus on others renders you clueless, and a failure to focus outward may leave you blindsided."

When it counts, don't let life's distractions—Facebook, your phone, the musings of malcontents—distract your Front Sight Focus. Don't fail to take into account the larger landscape, either. Process your next target. Focus. And then take aim at your target, whether a product launch or a sales goal.

MEN WITH
GREEN FACES

T HE ABILITY TO STRIKE fear in the hearts of your enemy is a
tremendous advantage for a SEAL.

In Vietnam, the Viet Cong called us "the men with green faces,"
because SEALs seemed to just rise up out of the ground without
warning. The speed and power of our actions were legendary.

If a SEAL team walked into an ambush—a favored tactic of the
enemy at that time—they did the opposite of what the enemy expected, and what others in the armed forces might have done. SEALs
ran full force straight at the enemy. Their actions saved lives, as op-
posed to ducking for cover inside an enemy's well-prepared kill box.
It is that mindset that makes the enemy fear the Navy SEALs. We
attack. We attack. And we attack.

SEALs exude what we call "Command Presence." Having Command Presence is both a physical and psychological trait. It is reflected in how confidently we stand, how purposefully we walk, and
how authoritatively we talk. Before we ever pull a trigger, our actions
convey our professionalism, confidence, and competence.

In the corporate world, dressing for success can be a key com-
ponent of such presence and professionalism. Your clothes convey
a powerful statement of you as a professional. Rightly or not, the

perceptions of your "audience" often determine their level of respect for you.

The popular online columnist for AskMen.com, "Mr. Mafioso," puts it in succinct SEAL-like language.

"Regardless of what you've done in the past, how much money you have in your bank account, how famous you are, or how fat you've become, a man in a well-tailored suit will always get treated better than some salami off the street," Mr. Mafioso says.

"I'm not talking about just any suit; I mean a well-fitted one, tailored by a man who left his village in the south of Italy to come to America with nothing but his needling skills and his shoes. This is not a time to be cheap. Get a suit that costs $200, and you'll look like $200. Get a suit that costs you $1,000, and you'll look like a million. And don't skimp on the shoes either; buy yourself one good pair at $400 a pop rather than four cheap pairs for $85."

Your clothing is often the first beachhead in corporate warfare. Tom, a forty-six-year-old software engineer and LUF graduate, tells me that while his teams may wear jeans and T-shirts at work when coding software, they dress to the nines when interacting with clients and potential partners.

"First impressions do count, regardless of how smart or knowledgeable you are," he said. "In the early days of my business, I know we lost contracts just because we came in to meetings looking like nerd-boys or granola-crunchers. We did not initially convey an image of being people you could trust or have confidence in. Just like your professional portfolio, a professional appearance establishes you as a serious person with credible and endless potential."

Of course, it's not just how you look. What matters just as much is how you carry yourself.

When you watch a SEAL team in action, their movement is fluid and deliberate; it shows Command Presence. And that speaks volumes. We believe that the first level of force is presence; for a SEAL, our presence alone instills fear in others.

In combat, when the shots go off, the first thing everybody does is drop their head. That's how we instinctually protect ourselves. It's no different in the real world. If a car backfires, or a firework explodes when we're not expecting it, we all jump and duck our heads. In both cases, the time between jumping and responding is decided by how well we overcome our fear.

Don't be fearful. Be fearless. Take the action. Hold your head high and attack.

NO LIMITS

ASK THE AVERAGE MAN on the street how many push-ups he can do and you'll likely get a straight answer. While striving to be honest and, at the same time, burnish his ego, he'll think for a moment and then say something like "I can do twenty-five." Or "I can knock out forty." A straight shooter.

Ask that same question of a Navy SEAL and you'll get a much different response: "I can do *at least* one hundred." And therein lies the ethos of a SEAL—we think in terms of possibilities, not limitations.

When you set hard numbers, you draw a line in the sand. You impose a self-limiting barrier between yourself and your untapped potential. If a man says he can do twenty-five push-ups, he'll likely stop when he gets to twenty-five, or close to it, basking in the accomplishment. Even if he goes over that number, he'll soon stop, because he knows he's already reached his goal or stated expectation. In his mind, he's done what he set out to do.

SEALs believe that the only limitations we have are those we place upon ourselves. That's why a SEAL will say, "I can do *at least*" whatever the number, and then start banging them out—going full bore to the point of exhaustion. We charge all out to a higher standard, not a limitation. And we won't be counting reps along the way, incidentally. We'll just go until we can't go anymore, exhausted from a Herculean effort. It's how we roll. If we don't attack challenges in that way, we know our teammates will rightly ask, "Is that seriously all you've got?" Or "Why didn't you keep going?" In other words, why did you quit when you had something left in the tank? You only have to go to failure once to prove to yourself and everyone else that you gave it your all, whatever the outcome.

At the same time, SEALs know that self-awareness is a gift from God. Some limitations are obvious and understandable. But we never put limits on ourselves; we know the enemy will do that for us. But they do so at their peril. We never bet against ourselves.

Several years ago, Theresa, the president of a software development firm in Southern California, attended one of my early seminars. She took the "no limits" mentality to heart, and decided to infuse it back in the office. She hired me to come coach her employees at the company's headquarters.

"I learned a new attitude and mindset about setting our corporate goals and achieving success," she told me. "For years, for me, setting goals was always about a specific number. We always translated a sales goal to a specific number with a plus or minus attached. After enduring everything the SEALs had to throw at me—and learning I had the capacity to do so much more than I ever thought possible—I changed my corporate mentality as well. Today, when we set sales goals we begin with 'At a minimum, we will achieve XXX.' It may sound like a small difference, but it evokes a mindset and a culture that's infectious across the staff. We bust that minimum all the time now because we don't put limits on ourselves."

It's the same for more mundane tasks. If you say you'll make 10 sales calls today, make 11, or 12, or 15. If you say you have a 95 percent defect-free policy, make it a zero-tolerance policy. Make every goal a stretch goal.

I'm convinced that if every business in America pushed just 10 percent harder today—just for one day—our economy would roar to full recovery in short order.

IF YOU'RE NOT CHEATING, YOU'RE NOT TRYING

SOMETIMES, YOUR BEST simply isn't good enough. That's the time a fellow SEAL will look you in the eye and say, "That's not getting it done. What else ya got?"

As a result, SEALs demand innovation and creativity. We foster and facilitate such a culture because our very lives can often depend on it. Doing so requires we be thoughtful and have the self-discipline to seek constant personal improvement. Why? Because we know that people—and our minds—win wars. Not machines.

Whether fashioning snowshoes out of swim fins during a cold-weather training exercise gone awry, or using a commercial calling card to order in air strikes when regular communications equipment fails, the adaptive, field-expedient capabilities of Navy SEALs are among our raison d'être.

In Haiti, in the early 1990s, SEALs armored up our own Humvees—we pieced together our own ballistic armor. We modified our pistols to provide better close-combat capabilities. None of this is classified information—just tactically necessary! We turbocharged our vehicles when it became clear that the factory setting wasn't fast enough.

SEALs don't wait around for organizational updates or standard-issue timelines. We can't. We modify training, tactics, and procedures to real-time circumstances and requirements. We harness the hard-earned "lessons learned" from fellow SEALs and their operations. Our lean, nimble, decentralized organization facilitates such quick creativity and innovation.

"Agility and innovation are the hallmarks of a great business," said Leo, a consultant and technology transfer entrepreneur I spoke with in 2014 regarding the need for nimbleness and adaptability in business endeavors. Because Leo and his employees provide recommendations that help governments modernize their policies, they must continually be on the cutting edge of technology, and find ways to champion and adapt its uses. Only then can they help their clients empower and protect consumers, promote competition, and ensure the resiliency and reliability of networks—the very things their clients publicly promise and demand.

"Like the SEALs, my business can't wait for time or chance. We're always pressing forward with new and innovative ideas and concepts. It's the lifeblood of our firm," he said. "We help others see the future and the possibilities.

"For example, I distinctly remember a famous photo graphic that was rampant on social media in 2013. It was a side-by-side comparison of news photos taken in 2005 and 2013 when Pope Benedict XVI and Pope Francis, respectively, were unveiled to the world. Both images show a sea of faithful Catholics jammed shoulder to shoulder in St. Peter's Square as they wait to witness the new pontiff. In the 2005 photo, one lone person in the back of the crowd hoists a flip phone and snaps a photo. Remember, this was still two years before the iPhone came onto the market and smartphone technology became rampant. In the 2013 image, AP photographer Michael Sohn captured a much different image. His photo shows a crowd that's awash in the glow of thousands of smartphone screens and tablet devices. Every person in the massive crowd seemed to have a smartphone! The technological revolution on display was breathtaking and revealing. Consumers can't wait to embrace new technologies to improve their lives and careers. Business owners must meet that demand.

"I show those images to my staff and to clients in order to illustrate both our love of computing power and connectivity and, even more importantly, our need to innovate, adapt, and transform in order to stay relevant in our marketplace and a continually-changing world. We've got to fight every day to stay ahead."

SEALs like to say, "If you're not cheating, you're not trying." It's not a rallying cry for illegal activity. It just means that we're constantly searching for innovative ways to stick it to the enemy. We'll fight dirty when called for and use every competitive advantage we can to get an edge. We know our enemies will never play fair—there are no fair fights in our business. There are none in yours, either. Do what it takes, while staying within the law.

OBSERVE, ORIENT, DECIDE, ACT— THE OODA LOOP

I N COMBAT, speed is a force multiplier.

But speed alone does not win battles. To emerge victorious, a SEAL must also continually outthink and out-execute his opponents. And he must do so not only with blinding speed but also with audacity. It's this combination that spells success because, in the end, whoever can handle the quickest rate of change is the one who survives.

SEALs are masters of maneuver warfare. They quickly decode complex environments before their enemies do, taking decisive action and exploiting the confusion their initiatives invariably cause. And then they confuse some more. They defeat their rivals by responding to rapidly changing conditions over which they have no control. Their agility is endless. They adapt. They improvise. They overcome.

To achieve this state, SEALs employ the prescient tactics of the brilliant military strategist John Boyd, a former Air Force fighter pilot and dogma-busting Pentagon consultant in the late twentieth century. Boyd's musings on how fighter pilots employ rapid assessment and adaptation skills to win dogfights transcend the cockpit and are applicable in any competitive endeavor. SEALs use what Boyd termed the "OODA Loop" concept to hone their tactical decision-making skills, giving them superior competitive advantage.

According to Boyd's concept, decision-making takes place in a recurring, interacting cycle of Observe, Orient, Decide, and Act. Whoever can synthesize this cycle more quickly—and ideally even "get inside" their enemy's own decision-making loop—will outmaneuver their opponents and ensure success. When done seamlessly, these maneuvers appear ambiguous to the enemy, generating confusion and disorder—yet another combat multiplier.

Boyd posited that all decisions are based on raw Observations, which are, in turn, processed via individual Orientation. Boyd contends that Orientation is the most important part of the OODA Loop since it shapes the way we observe, the way we decide, and the way we act. For SEALs, Orientation is informed by our experiences, culture, and exhaustive training. Because we spend two years training SEALs before we ever assign them to a team, SEALs are able to make more informed and intelligent decisions, based on rapid Observation and Orientation. Only then do we Act. And more often than not, we do it faster than the bad guys. As Boyd directs, we "continue the whirl of reorientation, mismatches, and analyses/synthesis over and over again ad infinitum." We adapt what we've learned in tandem with any new information that presents itself, applying new mental patterns to new situations. We're constantly observing—and interacting with—our combat environment, pulling things apart and putting them back together based on what's happening *now*.

SEALs know that speed, bravery, and toughness, while essential, are of little use without methodical deliberation. For us, the OODA Loop helps us in the decision-making process. And that's why we're the ones left standing.

YOU'LL KNOW
WHAT TO DO

O N JUNE 5, 1944, General George S. Patton delivered what historians consider one of the most rousing speeches ever given to a fighting force. If you've ever seen the movie *Patton,* you've heard the PG version delivered with passion by the actor George C. Scott. The speech was given in England to the Third US Army on the eve of the Allied invasion of France.

When I talk to business leaders about providing inspiration, direction, guidance, and hope to their charges, I can't help but reflect on Patton's powerful—if sometimes profane—words. For the general, profanity had its uses. According to the writer Charles M. Province, Patton had a unique ability regarding profanity. "During a normal conversation, he could liberally sprinkle four-letter words into what he was saying and the listeners would hardly take notice of it. He spoke so easily and used those words in such a way that it just seemed natural for him to talk that way. He could, when necessary, open up with both barrels and let forth such blue-flamed phrases that they seemed almost eloquent in their delivery."

Province wrote that once, when asked by his nephew about his profanity, Patton remarked, "When I want my men to remember something important, to really make it stick, I give it to them double dirty. It may not sound nice to some bunch of little old ladies at an afternoon tea party, but it helps my soldiers to remember. You can't run an army without profanity; and it has to be eloquent profanity. An army without profanity couldn't fight its way out of a piss-soaked paper bag. As for the types of comments I make, sometimes I just, by God, get carried away with my own eloquence."

Patton was a performer and deeply in love with his own image. But he was also a tremendously effective and inspirational leader. His men gladly followed him into hell. Luckily for most of us, we don't have to sail into Normandy or fight for Bastogneto to be inspired by George Patton. Here, according to most experts, is a portion of what Patton said to his troops on the eve of the Normandy invasion:

Be Seated:

Men, this stuff that some sources sling around about America wanting out of this war, not wanting to fight, is a crock of bullshit. Americans love to fight, traditionally. All real Americans love the sting and clash of battle.

You are here today for three reasons. First, because you are here to defend your homes and your loved ones. Second, you are here for your own self respect, because you would not want to be anywhere else. Third, you are here because you are real men and all real men like to fight.

When you, here, every one of you, were kids, you all admired the champion marble player, the fastest runner, the toughest boxer, the big league ball players, and the All-American football players. Americans love a winner. . . .

You are not all going to die. Only two percent of you right here today would die in a major battle. Death must not be feared. Death, in time, comes to all men. Yes, every man is scared in his first battle. If he says he's not, he's a liar. Some men are cowards but they fight the same as the brave men or they get the hell slammed out of them watching men fight who are just as scared as they are.

The real hero is the man who fights even though he is scared. Some men get over their fright in a minute under fire. For some, it takes an hour. For some, it takes days. But a real man will never let his fear of death overpower his honor, his sense of duty to his country, and his innate manhood. Battle is the most magnificent competition in which a human being can indulge. It brings out all that is best and it removes all that is base. Americans pride themselves on being He Men and they *are* He Men.

Remember that the enemy is just as frightened as you are, and probably more so. They are not supermen.

All through your Army careers, you men have bitched about what you call "chicken-shit drilling." That, like everything else in this Army, has a definite purpose. That purpose is alertness. Alertness must be bred into every soldier. I don't give a fuck for a man who's not always on his toes. You men are veterans or you wouldn't be here. You are ready for what's to come. A man must be alert at all times if he expects to stay alive. If you're not alert, sometime, a German son-of-an-asshole-bitch is going to sneak up behind you and beat you to death with a sock full of shit!

There are four hundred neatly marked graves somewhere in Sicily, all because one man went to sleep on the job. But they are German graves, because we caught the bastard asleep before they did.

An Army is a team. It lives, sleeps, eats, and fights as a team.

This individual heroic stuff is pure horse shit. The bilious bastards who write that kind of stuff for the *Saturday Evening Post* don't know any more about real fighting under fire than they know about fucking! We have the finest food, the finest equipment, the best spirit, and the best men in the world. Why, by God, I actually pity those poor sons-of-bitches we're going up against. By God, I do.

My men don't surrender, and I don't want to hear of any soldier under my command being captured unless he has been hit. Even if you are hit, you can still fight back. That's not just bullshit either. The kind of man that I want in my command is just like the lieutenant in Libya, who, with a Luger against his chest, jerked off his helmet, swept the gun aside with one hand, and busted the hell out of the Kraut with his helmet. Then he jumped on the gun and went out and killed another German before they knew what the hell was coming off. And, all of that time, this man had a bullet through a lung. There was a real man!

All of the real heroes are not storybook combat fighters, either. Every single man in this Army plays a vital role. Don't ever let up. Don't ever think that your job is unimportant. Every man has a job to do and he must do it. Every man is a vital link in the great chain.

What if every truck driver suddenly decided that he didn't like the whine of those shells overhead, turned yellow, and jumped headlong into a ditch? The cowardly bastard could say, "Hell, they won't miss me, just one man in thousands." But, what if every man thought that way? Where in the hell would we be now? What would our country, our loved ones, our homes, even the world, be like?

No, Goddamnit, Americans don't think like that. Every man does his job. Every man serves the whole. Every department, every unit, is important in the vast scheme of this war. . . .

One of the bravest men that I ever saw was a fellow on top of a telegraph pole in the midst of a furious fire fight in Tunisia. I stopped and asked what the hell he was doing up there at a time like that. He answered, "Fixing the wire, Sir." I asked, "Isn't that a little unhealthy right about now?" He answered, "Yes Sir, but the Goddamned wire has to be fixed." I asked, "Don't those planes strafing the road bother you?" And he answered, "No, Sir, but you sure as hell do!" Now, there was a real man. A real soldier. There was a man who devoted all he had to his duty, no matter how seemingly insignificant his duty might appear at the time, no matter how great the odds.

And you should have seen those trucks on the road to Tunisia. Those drivers were magnificent. All day and all night they rolled over those son-of-a-bitching roads, never stopping, never faltering from their course, with shells bursting all around them all of the time. We got through on good old American guts. Many of those men drove for over forty consecutive hours. These men weren't combat men, but they were soldiers with a job to do. They did it, and in one hell of a way they did it. They were part of a team. Without team effort, without them, the fight would have been lost. All of the links in the chain pulled together and the chain became unbreakable. . . .

The quicker we clean up this Goddamned mess, the quicker we can take a little jaunt against the purple-pissing Japs and clean out their nest, too—before the Goddamned Marines get all of the credit.

Sure, we want to go home. We want this war over with. The quickest way to get it over with is to go get the bastards who started it. The quicker they are whipped, the quicker we can go home. The shortest way home is through Berlin and Tokyo. And when we get to Berlin I am personally going to shoot that paper hanging son-of-a-bitch Hitler. Just like I'd shoot a snake! . . . My men don't dig foxholes. I don't want them to. Foxholes only slow up an offensive. Keep moving. And don't give the enemy time to dig one either. We'll win this war, but we'll win it only by fighting and by showing the Germans that we've got more guts than they have; or ever will have. . . .

I don't want to get any messages saying, "I am holding my position." We are not holding a Goddamned thing. Let the Germans do that. We are advancing constantly and we are not interested in holding onto anything, except the enemy's balls. We are going to twist his balls and kick the living shit out of him all of the time.

Our basic plan of operation is to advance and to keep on advancing regardless of whether we have to go over, under, or through the enemy. We are going to go through him like crap through a goose; like shit through a tin horn!

From time to time there will be some complaints that we are pushing our people too hard. I don't give a good Goddamn about such complaints. I believe in the old and sound rule that an ounce of sweat will save a gallon of blood. The harder *we* push, the more Germans we will kill. The more Germans we kill, the fewer of our men will be killed. Pushing means fewer casualties. I want you all to remember that.

There is one great thing that you men will all be able to say after this war is over and you are home once again. You may be thankful that twenty years from now when you are sitting by the fireplace with your grandson on your knee and he asks you what you did in the great World War II, you *won't* have to cough, shift him to the other knee and say, "Well, your Granddaddy shoveled shit in Louisiana." No, Sir. You can look him straight in the eye and say, "Son, your Granddaddy rode with the Great Third Army and a Son-of-a-Goddamned-Bitch named Georgie Patton!"

That is all.

THE ONLY WAY
OUT IS THROUGH

FORMER US PRESIDENT and Rough Rider Teddy Roosevelt once served as the assistant secretary of the United States Navy. He's also one of the most inspiring leaders I've ever read about.

There's no doubt in my mind he would have made a great Navy SEAL.

Everything about Teddy Roosevelt exuded the kind of life and leadership philosophies that SEALs aspire to. Throughout his life, TR was aggressive, tenacious, and unapologetic in his quest to always do the right thing. He was unafraid, resolute, and loyal. He attacked head-on the enormous challenges life threw his way, and willed himself to a better result. He epitomized the very essence of a fighter.

Born, as biographer Nathan Miller put it, a "puny, gangly lad with pipestem arms and legs—all speed, no strength," TR soon vowed as a very young child to physically re-create himself into the bull moose of a man he is remembered as. Despite an often crippling asthma condition, by age thirteen TR was camping in the Adirondacks, sleeping on the ground, shooting rapids, climbing mountains, and facing all the rigors of a wilderness woodsman. He conquered his physical ailments thanks in large part to his rigorous commitment.

Until his death at age sixty-one, the "Old Lion" pursued a vigor-

THE NAVY SEAL ART OF WAR

ous personal and professional life. He led combat troops into battle in the charge up Cuba's San Juan Hill, he was a rancher and sheriff in the South Dakota Badlands, and he was a trust-busting president who took on Wall Street's most powerful tycoons for the good of all Americans. He was an environmentalist and an author of American history. And he sailed up the Amazon into the rain forest. TR sucked the marrow out of life.

More important, he was mentally and physically fearless. Even if the battles we wage in this life end in defeat, TR felt, we should praise the individuals who are out there fighting them.

People "who spend themselves in a worthy cause," he believed, are the stuff of legend. Forget the cynical and selfish folks—those uninspired individuals who watch (and critique) life from the sidelines. Go get yours—whatever that means. You deserve it.

It is not the critic who counts; not the man who points out how the strong man stumbles, or where the doer of deeds could have done them better. The credit belongs to the man who is actually in the arena, whose face is marred by dust and sweat and blood; who strives valiantly; who errs, who comes short again and again, because there is no effort without error and shortcoming; but who does actually strive to do the deeds; who knows great enthusiasms, the great devotions; who spends himself in a worthy cause; who at the best knows in the end the triumph of high achievement, and who at the worst, if he fails, at least fails while daring greatly, so that his place shall never be with those cold and timid souls who neither know victory nor defeat.

—Theodore Roosevelt

TEAM ABILITY

SEALS EXPECT TO LEAD, but they are also willing to be led by someone with a better plan. In the absence of orders we take charge, leading our teammates and accomplishing the mission. But if, in the heat of battle, someone else on the team has a better extraction plan than the team leader, the team leader will defer to the other's expertise. That kind of "team ability" requires trust, confidence, and respect from every member of the team. It's also what makes SEAL teams so special and effective. Rank may have its privileges, but it's usually moot on operations.

Those who think they always know what's right or, even worse, what's best, make poor teammates and bad leaders. That's especially true if the person leading starts dictating. A successful SEAL learns early on the value of teamwork and does his best to fit into the team and know his place and play his role, rather than try to bend it to his will or desires. A good leader may not always have the best ideas, for example, but he may be great at getting them from others. Confident in his abilities, he doesn't need to conquer or dominate the group. If he's a genuine professional, others will quickly recognize it and respect his authority.

I find the notion of team before self resonates with my clients, the executives I work with. They understand and value a culture of teamwork. When you're in charge of an organization, it's easier to see the value of an orchestrated, team-focused approach to running a business.

Individuals, however, sometimes are unable to see things as clearly.

Randall was an extremely talented graphic artist at a major publishing company who found himself stuck in midlevel management positions, despite his attempts to secure a more senior one. I met him at a seminar I was giving in Washington, D.C., on the power of teamwork. He breathlessly sought me out after the speech and asked for my advice.

"My boss won't give me the promotion I deserve," he said, "and I can't figure out why. I've been patient and waited for opportunities to present themselves but when they do, I'm never the person picked for the promotion."

In the SEALs, we'd call him "One-Way Randall"—the guy who only cares about himself and his own needs.

I quickly discovered that Randall was also the guy who always raised his hand in staff meetings; he had an incessant need to be heard and to be seen as the smartest guy in the room. To him, advancement was about self-promotion, not mission accomplishment. Instead of encouraging others, or elevating the discussion, he preened and positioned himself in the best light possible in the hope that those above him would take notice. What he didn't know was that while others may have respected his skills, they found him personally insufferable. His boss noticed him all right. He saw Randall for exactly what he was: a terrific asset and performer, but not someone suited to lead a larger organization. He valued Randall's abilities, but never once considered him as a possible successor or even a number two. It wasn't until I described the sorts of behaviors that help SEALs thrive as a team that Randall understood how his behavior was impacting his career.

"I always thought I had to cut others off at the knees, to be seen as the go-to guy," he said. "I never once considered where I best fit in order to make the *organization* better. It was always about me, not the bigger team. I wonder where I'd be now if I'd realized that years ago."

As Randall discovered, the SEALs have mastered the art of getting along with others. It's an essential skill among a bunch of dynamic, Type A individuals working in a high-pressure group environment. But, as a result of our ability to get along, and always act with the team's welfare and success in mind, we're a very formidable opponent.

We also know that our "team" includes far more than just the trigger pullers. SEALs do not write checks. We don't order maps, optics, or ammo. We don't provide or fix our own guns. We get the glory, but nothing happens without the Air Force pilots who deliver us to the landing zone (or LZ), or the Navy Special Boat Teams and their combatant crewmen who pluck us out of harm's way. For every SEAL there are eight to ten others who support us. Whatever our job or position, we do well to never forget that everyone on the team is important.

Stephen is the chief medical officer at a hospital association in the Southwest. It's his job to improve quality, reduce costs, and improve the health of his association's patient population. After going through a training event with us in 2012 and discovering the power of teamwork, Stephen led a cultural revolution at his hospital group that continues to yield benefits and improve profits. He reminded his staff that everyone was important and had much to contribute to the "mission" of patient care, whether they were a nurse or a brain surgeon. And everyone was to be treated with dignity and respect.

"In the operating room, for example, many nurses felt that some doctors didn't understand, respect, or care to listen to their views on patient care," Stephen said. "Even worse, some doctors were rude, dismissive, or even intimidating [in dealing with] the nursing staff. Corporately, we made a commitment to improve the relationship aspects in our hospitals. We empowered nurses to speak their minds without fear of reprisal. We counseled our doctors to treat others they work with with more dignity and respect. The results have been incredible."

Stephen said that from empowering the nurses and creating a more collaborative working environment, incidents of operating room errors, accidents, and unnecessary treatment have plummeted and patient care has markedly improved. Morale among the staffs has soared and the bottom line (thanks to fewer patient lawsuits) has improved.

There's a good chance that someone out there might be better than me at a given task, but better than my SEAL team? Not likely. No doubt it will be the same for your team, too.

THE ONLY EASY DAY
WAS YESTERDAY

IT IS IMPERATIVE that we live in the moment. What we do right now, this moment, is what ultimately matters.

SEALs know that the only easy day was *yesterday,* because that day is *over.* Today's mission will most likely deliver new and unimagined challenges and difficulties. Consequently, we never rest on laurels, because we fervently believe that what happened yesterday no longer counts.

Dan Antonelli is the CEO and creative director of New Jersey advertising agency Graphic D-Signs Inc. as well as the author of *Building a Big Small Business Brand.* In a recent article in *Entrepreneur* magazine, Antonelli described what happens when business owners are blinded by their past successes and can't see beyond their ego.

"They get beat out by those hungry for strategic expertise that will move them to the next stage," Antonelli said. "These 'Mediocre Business Owners' rationalize past success as a justification for today's complacency. Unfortunately, this lack of proactive planning often returns to haunt them. Successful business owners don't rest on their laurels. They keep an eye on competitors, pursue innovation and get help when they need it."

Antonelli argues that, in some cases, the mediocre business owner avoids or fears change. Even worse, they refute the advice of others—including their own customers!

"After all, why fix it if it isn't broken?" he says. "They worry that reinventing their (mediocre) brand identity might confuse customers and negatively impact their business. They hesitate to adopt new technology because it's an unknown. They pour thousands into their old Yellow Pages ad because 'it worked before.' As a result, they maintain the status quo, rather than embracing the ideas offered by qualified professionals and business mentors."

As SEALs, we know that yesterday's success—as great as it might have been—is just that. But we also know today brings new challenges and opportunity for even greater success. But it requires our full attention, innovation, and devotion. That's why we put it all on the table today, right here, right now; yesterday is history and tomorrow may never come.

There's real excitement and nobility in facing new challenges every day. Don't be one of those timid and regretful "woulda, coulda, shoulda" souls. Don't *wish* you would have done more when your moment came. Know it now.

THE POWER OF
PATIENCE

I N THE REAL WORLD, patience is a virtue. On the battlefield, it can be an actual weapons system. Hard-charging, dynamic individuals like Navy SEALs thrive in what are known as kinetic operations: full-auto, full-fury engagements. We see the hill. We take the hill. But successful SEALs know that instant gratification, while rewarding, is often unattainable and usually counterproductive.

SEAL snipers are among the most patient—and productive—warriors in America's arsenal. While stalking their prey clandestinely in ways a larger, conventional force could never do, snipers measure success in the inches they can silently advance over hours—days even—of effort. When perched atop a building, providing watch over maneuvering forces on the ground, snipers take out unsuspecting threats before they present themselves, or use their detailed observation to convey actionable intelligence to their comrades on the streets below. Heat, cold, and discomfort are mere distractions that they never let hinder their quest. Their reward—one shot, one kill—is worth the wait.

Patience is not inaction. It is not laziness. It is not being slow. Individuals who exhibit patience know the right time to act. A patient warrior is in control of his emotions, actions, and desires. He demonstrates the intestinal fortitude to keep going, conquering one piece of ground at a time until the mission is a success. Even if that takes years. SEALs realize they don't always need to *get things done right now,* and that delaying an action doesn't equate to *wasting time or being indecisive.* Rather, it is reckless impatience that risks lives, goals, relationships, missions, even the battle or war.

One must wait for the target to present itself, wait for the wind and angles to properly align, wait for the optimal moment to squeeze the trigger and send the round downrange.

One must be slow when there's a need to be slow, and quick when there's a need to be quick. Focus on which method is best to accomplish a specific task.

It was Tolstoy who said, the two most powerful warriors are patience and time.

CLEAR, CONCISE
COMMUNICATION

I'M ABSOLUTELY CONVINCED of the value of clear, concise, specific communications. Whether you're issuing a Commander's Intent, negotiating a car purchase, or explaining the rules of basketball to your nine-year-old, the more direct and precise you can be in your language, the better the result.

As Sun Tzu said, "If words of command are not clear and distinct, if orders are not thoroughly understood, then the general is to blame. But, if orders are clear and the soldiers nevertheless disobey, then it is the fault of their officers."

The same can be said in your dealings with others: friends, business associates, family. Remember, good communication is an exercise in clear thinking.

Case in point, consider the secret message from former secretary of state Colin Powell to the Mullah Omar, the one-eyed former leader of Afghanistan and spiritual leader of the Taliban regime. Omar and the Taliban sheltered Osama bin Laden and his al-Qaida network in the years prior to the September 11, 2001, attacks.

In October 2001, on the eve of America's shock-and-awe invasion of Afghanistan, Powell sent a secret cable to the American embassy in Pakistan. The cable was unclassified on September 11, 2011, ten years after it was issued. In it, Powell directed Ambassador Wendy Chamberlin to leverage Pakistani intermediaries and deliver a private, hundred-word message to Omar. There was nothing wordy or diplomatic about the correspondence. There was certainly no indication that Powell longed for further dialogue. Powell simply told Omar that unless he handed over Osama bin Laden, "every pillar of the Taliban regime will be destroyed."

It was an exercise in crystal-clear communication.

10/05/01

From: Secretary of State
To: American Embassy, Islamabad

Eyes Only for Ambassador Chamberlin

1. Ambassador Chamberlin should seek immediate appointment with General Mahmud to request that either he or president Musharraf immediately deliver the following message to Mullah Omar.

2. Begin Message.

   – We have information that Al Qaida is planning additional terrorist acts.

   – If any person or group connected in any way to Afghanistan conducts a terrorist act against our country, our forces, or those of our friends or allies, our response will be devastating.

   – It is in your interest and in the interest of your survival to hand over all Al Qaida leaders, to close the terrorists' camps and allow the US access to terrorist facilities.

- We will hold leaders of the Taliban personally responsible for any such actions. Every pillar of the Taliban regime will be destroyed. (end message).

Powell

Just days after the message was delivered, Omar fled Kabul. And America invaded. Clearly, Omar got the message. By December 2001, the United States had driven the Taliban from power. Unfortunately, Mullah Omar remains at large and represents a continuing threat to America and her allies. And while no longer a government, the Taliban remain an insurgency movement, despite our devastating response.

IN THE ABSENCE OF
LEADERSHIP ... LEAD

I BELIEVE IN the African proverb "It takes a village." To me, the saying connotes teamwork and leadership. Unfortunately, there are plenty of idiots living in those villages, too, and you've got to account for them.

Let me give you an example. On a recent training exercise with thirty-five high-powered CEOs, it became clear that the man we'd tapped to be the class leader was in over his head. He was not leading his men—it was more like management by walking around; he certainly wasn't inspiring anyone. While this leader, let's call him Joe, had performed well in many other leadership roles, he was having a difficult time leading his charges on this particularly stressful, high-stakes exercise.

Our group was tasked with assaulting a group of suspected "terrorists" who were holed up inside an abandoned hospital. It provided our students and instructors the opportunity to evaluate the class's close-quarters combat skills. The students were told that "Pedro," a notorious bomb maker, was hiding inside the building along with his men. The bad guys were role players hired by me; they acted and dressed accordingly. The students' mission: assault the six-floor building in four eight-man teams and neutralize the problem. The class leader would coordinate the teams and the attack, conveying orders and direction.

It was an eerie evolution. The building was an abandoned hospital that I had rented for the event. It was dark, cavernous, and filled with hundreds of rooms and other places for bad guys to hide in and attack from. The only light came from the emergency floodlights and hall-way indicators—the sort of lighting you see when main power sources are severed. Our teams were told to move in coordinated fashion to sweep the entire hospital looking for Pedro and his posse. They had to clear rooms and hallways and, when necessary, engage active shoot-ers with their plastic-BB-firing airsoft rifles. It was a tough task even for seasoned SEALs, and it was extremely tense and scary for our stu-dent teams.

Unfortunately, the situation went from tense to inept because the class leader abdicated his leadership responsibilities. He remained in the rear, giving him no situational awareness, and he wilted when things started going south. Instead of working hard to coordinate and lead the multi-team attack, he seemed satisfied to simply watch things unfold from afar. Before long, he watched things quickly fall apart.

The teams were attacked by roaming, gun-toting terrorists who would shoot and run and then hide and wait. The initial assault plans—as usually happens after first contact with a motivated enemy— were scrapped as individual teams scattered. Teams that were sup-posed to be on the third floor ran to the fifth. Friendly-fire incidents were rampant. The students began to be mowed down en masse in ambush after ambush. Unit discipline and integrity fell by the way-side as individual team members sought to save themselves, breaking ranks and bolting in every direction. Communications were nonexis-tent. No one was in charge.

When things were at their worst, one of my instructors stood up on a crate in a hallway jam-packed with jittery, rifle-toting students, each heading down the hallway in different directions, and yelled:

"WHO'S IN CHARGE HERE?!" No one answered. "WHO'S IN CHARGE?!" he repeated. Again, no answer—just blank stares from the students. That's because no one—not the class leader, not the team leaders—was in charge. And no one seemed to want the job. It turned out that Joe was at the other end of the same hallway, squawking on a walkie-talkie to a team leader who was just ten feet away! He was following a group of students, ostensibly trying to achieve some situational awareness. In fact, he was just clueless. He didn't even respond when my instructor yelled "WHO'S IN CHARGE?!" He seemed afraid to own it.

My instructor looked in disbelief at this group of hard-charging, Type A executives and offered this universal SEAL maxim: "In the absence of leadership . . . LEAD!" His point was clear—somebody has to pick up the flag and drive the mission forward. When no one is in charge, someone has to *take* charge.

I'm not suggesting a bloodless coup or revolt. This is about filling a vacuum. On many SEAL missions I was on, for many different reasons (injuries, geographical separation, mental trauma), our leader was taken out of the fight. When that happened, the next-best qualified teammate unhesitatingly stepped up and took command.

Quality leadership is essential to any mission success. But it requires individual leaders to drive it.

THE LEADERSHIP
QUARTET

I'M CONVINCED THAT the very best leaders deliver the following quartet:

1. Inspiration

2. Direction

3. Guidance

4. Hope

Over the years, in uniform and out, I've learned that these four qualities are ingrained in every effective leader. Let me break them out for you.

INSPIRATION

A pretty simple concept. You inspire others. You inspire them, as John Quincy Adams once said, to dream more, learn more, do more, and become more. I'm not talking about being charismatic, though that always helps. I'm talking about being the sort of person that others want to be like, and are willing to follow. SEALs do that by being experienced experts at their craft; having vision, enthusiasm, and passion. They inspire by being ethical and principled and in being responsible and accountable for the mission and their actions. If you inspire me, you motivate me. That's an awesome combination.

DIRECTION

In any organization, it's the leader's job to ensure that everyone is on the same page. They provide crystal-clear direction. In SEAL terms, it means delivering the Commander's Intent.

Direction and intent ensures that everyone understands the organization's mission as well as its purpose. It includes goals and objectives, roles and responsibilities, and individual performance expectations. It indicates deadlines and critical metrics and gates. It helps everyone on the team—whether they are a sniper, a breacher, a boat driver, or a demolitions expert—to understand how their individual job fits into the larger strategic picture.

GUIDANCE

Once leaders deliver the direction, they must then provide the proper guidance to help get the job done. More important, by guiding or mentoring others, a leader helps their team members or employees become the best they can be. This does not mean doing the other person's work. It means the leader leverages his or her expertise to help develop the other person. Guidance still involves articulating direction, but it also means giving guidance and advice and being supportive. It means serving as a role model and protecting the other person to the extent possible. It means providing opportunities and opening doors. It means caring for and feeding another.

HOPE

Hope may not be a method—or a strategy—but it is something everyone craves. It's also something a leader of an organization can actually give.

On many an operation, things have seemed pretty bleak to me. I've often wondered if the juice was worth the squeeze—if we'd make it out alive and whether or not anyone at headquarters really cared about our sorry asses. I have no doubt many employees feel the same way at times at their own companies. When a leader gives others hope, they're telling their people that things will get better, or that those things are not as bad as they may seem. They remind us that what we're doing means something and is not for naught. Hope conveys confidence. And is infectious. And when people have hope, they are willing to commit.

But hope has an admission price: trust. A leader must have the trust and confidence of his employees before hope can be transferred. Without trust, hopeful words are simply that.

THE IMPORTANCE
OF TRUST

*I knew wherever I was that you thought of me, and if
I got in a tight place you would come, if alive.*

—General William T. Sherman to General Ulysses S. Grant

I LOVE THIS SIMPLE NOTE from Sherman to Grant. It spoke of
the remarkable bond of trust between two military men—a bond
that is the very bedrock of what it means to be a SEAL team member.

Without trust, there is no SEAL team. Some people think I am
crazy to consider entering a smoke-filled room filled with bad guys
with guns who want to shoot me. But I do it with gusto because I trust
my teammates. And because of that trust, the attack can proceed. I
can't do my job—clear the left side of the room—unless I can trust
that the guy coming in right behind me will do his job and clear the
right side. We trust and rely on each other.

Just to be clear, it takes a tremendous amount of discipline not to
look to the right when I am clearing my left-side space. But that's the

beauty—and the benefit—of trust. And it's funny—with trust comes success.

For the record, there are plenty of guys I didn't like or could not stand on my Teams. But I trusted them. I trusted their professionalism and talents. Through the prism of shared adversity and experiences, I grew to have faith in the competence, integrity, and motivation of my fellow SEALs and our leaders. Thanks to open communication and demonstrated commitment, we shared the same values and goals. Because of that, we formed bonds of trust, if not always friendships. I learned early on that if I didn't have such a bond with the team-mates and leaders I counted on for success, operations would come to a crashing—perhaps deadly—halt.

And sometimes I learned, as Ernest Hemingway said, that some-times the best way to learn if I could trust somebody was to trust them, until they gave me a reason not to.

When I talk about trust with the business executives I work with, I'm more and more convinced that it is a universal value. The most successful clients know trust is a valuable business commodity. Like the SEAL stranded on a mountaintop surrounded by enemy fighters who trusts that air support will come when he calls for it, employees must trust that their employer—their team or divisional leaders—will look out for them. That if everything starts falling apart, they won't be left behind. If a bond of sacred trusts exists, people are willing to take risks, to stand and fight, to go the extra mile—all without being asked. If they don't have trust, they do only what's expected and little more. They play it safe. They think only of them-selves. If a company's customers don't trust that it will deliver on its products and promises, they'll head for the nearest competitor at full speed.

So how do SEALs develop trust with one another and with other organizations? Here are just a few of the ways:

- We live a culture of honesty and integrity. Those things actually matter to us.

- We keep promises and don't make them lightly.

- We value relationships and honor them.

- We involve the entire team in the decision-making process.

- We're loyal—to one another and to our team.

- It's never about us, but always about the mission.

- We share common goals and passionately pursue them.

- We're transparent. If we think you're full of shit, we'll tell you so. It's rarely personal; it's just business.

- If we need three helicopters to do a job, we need three helicopters. We don't inflate the statistics, or exaggerate the risks.

- We have a solid track record of proven past performance.

- We are committed to excellence in everything we do. And we can prove it. We walk the walk.

In 2012, the magazine *Fast Company* reported that companies with high levels of trust enjoy higher stock prices, improved profits, and better retention of key employees. Sounds like a SEAL team to me.

HAVE SERVANT'S HEART

THE BEST LEADERS I KNOW not only provide a tremendous service, but they also serve. They subordinate their own individual needs and desires to some greater good. For these leaders, the business, the employees, the customers, and the mission come well before self. They visibly, passionately care about the well-being of their charges. They have, in short, a servant's heart.

I was lucky to work with many servant leaders in my twenty years in the SEAL teams. Men who made it a point to care more about me on some god-awful mission in some godforsaken country than they did about themselves. Leaders who did small yet magnanimous things like making sure my teammates and I ate before they did, or got to use the last precious minutes of allotted satellite phone time to check in with a loved one—even if it meant they would miss out on talking to theirs. And these weren't one-time, grandstanding actions. They were emblematic of a true leadership style. It's who these leaders were. As a result, they had my loyalty and devotion. I would take a bullet for them if I had to. That's in sharp contrast to an ambassador I once had to protect while on a mission to Bosnia in the 1990s. This window-licker looked at the SEALs sent to protect him from potential assassins as the hired help. He preened and primped like a petulant peacock, barked orders to everyone, and obviously didn't give a rat's ass about any of us. In his mind, we were there to serve him. Well, he may have been a hell of a diplomat in a war-torn world, but he was an arrogant ass as a person. I can't help but think he was the main reason our diplomatic efforts suffered and struggled so much. On one particularly dangerous day, as we shuttled him from one hot spot to the next, I remember him looking at me and seriously saying, "We both know your job is to take a bullet for me if need be, chief." After choking back a less diplomatic response, I looked him square in the eye and said, "No, sir. My job is to kill the bastard who kills you." You reap what you sow.

In SEAL teams, we train leaders who focus primarily on the growth and well-being of their teammates, in addition to carrying out the mission. It's a big part of why we're so efficient and successful. Because we are not a top-down, hierarchical organization, we share power, put the needs of fellow SEALs first, and continually ensure our people are being properly developed and performing as highly as possible. We embrace collaboration and thrive on trust. We are humble and trustworthy. We believe in honor and respect. None of us is trying to screw the other and take their place on some corporate ladder. We're all climbing it together. For each of us, it's about leadership and accomplishing a noble mission, not increasing our own personal power.

As a result, we are driven by values and the well-being of others. We genuinely see the value in—and reap the benefits of—putting other people first. Make no mistake, this sort of approach in no way connotes a weak or soft, sappy style. Just because a leader prioritizes the others they serve doesn't mean you can get over on them. In fact, some of the best servant leaders I know and worked for were some of the toughest and most demanding sons of bitches I have ever laid eyes on.

It's much the same in the civilian world. In his bestselling book

Good to Great: Why Some Companies Make the Leap and Others Don't, author and business consultant Jim Collins studied more than 1,400 companies and selected what he described as eleven truly great ones. Companies like Gillette, Kroger, and Walgreen's were among the eleven that transitioned from being average to being truly great, based on financial performance over a sustained period of time. Part of their ability to make the leap was due in large measure to the leadership styles of their corporate bosses.

According to Collins, each of these CEOs was a "level five" or servant-type leader, a person who possessed characteristics like humility and self-awareness. They are the sorts of people who shun personal glory and who glean greater satisfaction from solving problems and helping others than they do in heaping praise and honors on themselves. Collins discovered that companies with servant-type leaders are more results oriented and achieve more sustainable periods of exceptional performance than their competitors.

Collins found out what SEALs have known for a long time: that being a selfless, team-focused player who constantly strives for self-improvement is what drives ultimate mission success.

At SOT-G, I always promise my clients that we'll provide a tremendous service, and that we'll also serve. We will serve their needs, their desires; it's all about them and not our own ambitions. And guess what, we both win in the end.

While the SEALs have hammered that notion home to me, it was my mother who first taught me about the dignity and nobility of service. Divorced, with six kids to raise, she spent most of her working life—nearly thirty years—as a second-shift cleaning lady in a hospital. But she was so much more than that. At work, she was a confidante to the nurses and a comfort to the patients. She was a rock of compassion for her coworkers and a reality check for the surgeons. She gave of herself each and every day to others. And at her funeral wake, the line to get into the funeral home stretched for what seemed like miles. A planned two-hour wake soon turned into a seven-hour procession and celebration.

Until that day, I honestly had no idea how much love she had for the people at her hospital—and the love and gratitude they had for her. Her death, one coworker said, "felt like someone had ripped the soul out of the hospital." She was a community leader in every sense of the term. People in suits and scrubs, young and old—from the most senior hospital administrator to the parking lot attendant—came that day to pay their respects to this Christian servant. A woman and mother who lived her life as a noble servant but who was anything but a servile cleaning lady. I was proud and amazed.

Whenever I need a humility check, or start thinking I'm the most important person on the team, I always remember my mom, and the words of Lao Tzu, the ancient Chinese philosopher who was a contemporary of the military strategist Sun Tzu. In addition to putting me back in my place, it reminds me that SEALs don't have a monopoly on great ideas.

A leader is best when people barely know that he exists, not so good when people obey and acclaim him, worst when they despise him. Fail to honor people, they fail to honor you. But of a good leader, who talks little, when his work is done, his aims fulfilled, they will all say, "We did this ourselves."

COME TO THE
EDGE. AND FLY.

I F THERE IS one universal truth that binds all Navy SEALs, it's that BUD/S showed us we could accomplish more than we ever thought possible. We could run farther and faster than we ever imagined, lift more logs than we could ever count, endure any and every physical and mental torture the Navy could toss at us. All that was required was a belief in ourselves. That and a willing attitude, some physical output, and a few motivated—if depraved—instructors.

Ask any SEAL and they'll tell you the same thing. The transformative moment happens in different ways at different times for different people but, eventually, we all transform. We embrace the belief that nothing is impossible if we are willing to give what it takes to make it so. While there may be apprehension, there is no fear. It involves mental, physical, and emotional release. Not everyone, however, is strong enough physically and mentally, or brave enough to commit. They are unwilling to see what's possible, and as a result limit their unlimited potential.

Stephen is one of the fearless souls. After spending two summers with me and my teams in various events, he claims nothing scares him anymore. Even the idea of merging his plastics manufacturing company with a slightly larger rival, or regularly inviting his customers to grade the performance of his teams and the quality of their products. To him, these are existential actions that a leader must often take.

"I know many companies that refuse to conduct customer surveys because they are afraid of what people will say," he said. "I am not afraid of possible negative results and neither are my top managers. We believe in taking responsibility and learning from our mistakes."

When he decided to merge his company with a slightly larger rival, he did not fear the churn that resulted. Instead, he used it as an opportunity to grow the business.

"Organizations and markets change all the time," he said. "You can't get stuck in the past. You can cherish the past, but you've got to fearlessly focus on the future."

In that same spirit, I'm a huge fan of a simple, twenty-seven-word poem by the British poet, playwright, and screenwriter Christopher Logue called "Come to the Edge." I once saw it on a poster in a library and have never forgotten it. It captures something I see every day in the leaders I am trying to develop: a fear of flying. I also see a little of myself in the verses. I am the "pusher."

I never met Logue, but am told he was a devout pacifist. Despite the differences in our worldviews, I'm confident we could have shared a beer or two, and enjoyed talking endlessly about the power of untapped potential.

Come to the edge.
We might fall.
Come to the edge.
It's too high!
COME TO THE EDGE!
And they came
And he pushed
And they flew.

Are you still standing on an edge, just waiting for a push? Are you too comfortable, too scared, too busy, too ... anything? It's tragic how many people hold on to what they know—bad relationships, dead-end jobs, uninspiring lives, stifled dreams—because they fear the unknown. Each of us has near-limitless possibilities, but you've got to be willing to put your balls on the table now and again and take the chance they'll be whacked.

At the same time, dynamic leaders must invest the time and energy to push others along on their paths to greatness. That's your job—to make them believe in themselves and their potential. When you see the light go off, it's a beautiful thing.

Stop waiting at the edge. Consider yourself pushed.

JUST ONE MORE

WHEN WAS THE LAST TIME you told yourself, "Just one more"? I don't care what it was—a push-up, a bench press, another practice swing, a piggyback ride with your child, another attack at a seemingly impossible problem. When was the last time you willed yourself to go once more, into the breach, and give it something extra? If you're like most people, it doesn't happen very often. Comfort and familiarity are habits.

So today, commit to doing "just one more" of something—and that's after you've already given it your all. One more rep. One more lap. One more mile. One more piggyback ride. Dig down deep, grab hold, and push it out. You'll begin to create new and better habits of excellence and performance. And you will continually expand your capabilities.

THERE IS NO
FINISH LINE

INSTEAD OF LOOKING for the finish line, tell yourself there is no such thing. Instead, constantly immerse yourself in (and learn from) the journey. And continually be prepared for what's just around the corner.

In my seminars—just as it was for us in the SEALs—I'm known for constantly reminding people that there is no finish line, whatever it is that you might be doing. I don't care if you're on a training run, lifting weights, or celebrating the completion of an important project. If someone has their eye and mind on the finish line or, worse yet, believes they have actually crossed it, they are at grave risk of losing the race. That's because they'll let their guard down and allow someone stronger, smarter, or faster to snatch the prize.

There are always new challenges to face, more things to accomplish, higher mountains to climb, or harder targets to attack. When you strive for excellence in all things, there's little room for emotional or physical peaks and valleys. It's best to train your mind and your bodies to stay on top, at all times, and keep pressing forward. In BUD/S training, for example, instructors rarely tell trainees how long a run or forced march will be. If they do, they often derail that train when the designated distance is achieved. I do the same with my corporate clients. The concept behind such actions is simple. We want SEALs to be like Energizer bunnies: to keep going and going and going, until the going is done—whenever that is. And without them ever knowing when that is. We want their full attention and full effort every step of the way regardless of how many steps we have to take together.

Most people can't step off unless they know where the finish line is. For some reason, they equate their ability to accomplish a task with knowing how long or far they must go. It's better to just step off with the mindset that you'll go as far and as long as you can go and only stop when you can't go any more. And then you'll take a rest, and get up and go some more.

Stop asking where the finish line is, or when we'll be done, or if we've given enough effort to whatever it is that we're doing. It will be over when it's over and not one second before. To be successful in everything you do, it's essential you wrap your head around this concept.

Billionaire businessman and Microsoft cofounder Bill Gates, whose net worth in 2013 was estimated at $72 billion, doesn't believe in breaking the tape. When asked by *Playboy* magazine in 1994 if it was nothing less than industry domination that he had in mind, Gates responded:

> *But what does it mean to win? If I were a guy who just wanted to win, I would have already moved on to another arena. If I'd had some set idea of a finish line, don't you think I would have crossed it years ago?*

Be like Bill Gates. Stop looking for the finish line. Just run the race.

ARE YOU INJURED
OR ARE YOU HURT?

The BEST THING ABOUT PAIN is that it lets you know you aren't dead yet.

I've learned that lesson the hard way over the years and it rings especially true as you get older. Life brings pain—both emotional and physical—in all of our endeavors. There's no avoiding it. But how you *deal* with it—and what you do *with* it—is largely up to you.

SEALs like to say that pain is just weakness leaving the body. There's real truth in that slogan. If you can experience pain, walk into it head-on, and push your way past it, it can be a difficult but incredibly beneficial learning experience. I've learned how to live with pain, but more important, I don't use pain as an excuse to quit—at anything. We all experience pain in our everyday lives. But when you are able to carry on—to play through the pain—you become both more resilient and more respected.

All that said, there is a significant difference between hurting and being injured. It's important to never confuse the two. If you're injured, you're out. If you're hurting, you can still play. It's as simple as that. And while I'm mostly talking about the physical world, you can draw similar correlations to the emotional realm as well.

I put clients through tremendous physical challenges at my Leadership Under Fire events. Only when you push yourself to your limits can you really get to know yourself on a primal level. Among the things my clients experience are calisthenics, endless runs, ocean swims, close-quarters combat drills, martial arts training, and more. Invariably, someone is always hurting or injured. When that happens, my staff and I are quickly able to separate the lions from the lambs.

There was this one guy, a stocky dude in his early forties, who popped his shoulder out of its socket during a night swim in the Pacific. He'd gotten pounded by crazy surf and driven to the seafloor. He'd used his shoulder as a plow. He came out of the water, holding his right arm slightly away from his body, supporting the injured wing with his left hand. There was a noticeable bulge in front of his right shoulder joint, and he was clearly, visibly in pain. I knew immediately that he had dislocated the thing. He did, too. Unfortunately, he had missed out on the previous year's event because of a similar injury. He'd popped the shoulder just one week before the event and had to disenroll. He'd spent the next year training his ass off for this class.

Now, this guy was injured. No question about it. The last place he wanted to be was standing there on the beach and not in the cold, dark water. Still, we knew the injury was bad, so we quickly iced him up, crafted a makeshift sling out of a towel, and made plans for a medical evac to a San Diego hospital. His night swim was over, maybe even his LUF experience, through no fault of his own.

Not twenty minutes later, another fellow came out of the surf complaining that both his shoulders hurt. He was worried about the pain he was experiencing. He wasn't sure he ... *could go on.* My medical tech asked him where it hurt. "All over," he said with dramatic flourish. "Every time I lift my arms, it hurts like hell." He looked at the doc and then looked at me. And then he looked at the other instructors. He didn't like what he saw. He was met with impassive—downright impatient—faces. He liked what he heard even less. "Yeah, well, everybody's hurting. It's a painful thing." What he wanted was some empathy. He was looking for someone to tell him he'd done well and that it was okay to quit. That he'd given a great effort . . . that we understood his pain.

The problem was that we did understand his pain. He hurt. So what? You're supposed to hurt on a two-mile open-ocean swim. It's supposed to hurt when you're pushing your limits and comfort zone. That's the whole point. If it were easy and pain-free, everyone would be doing it.

Later that night, when everyone was out of the water and sitting around a campfire recounting the day's missions, I told the class about the difference between hurting and being injured.

When you're hurting, you feel pain. You are uncomfortable. Quite likely you'll see blood and bruises, cuts and tears. The difference, though, is that you can still perform if you are hurt. You can play through the pain. If you are hurt, you suck it up, walk it off, get back up, and keep going.

Injured, conversely, means you are done; out, over, sidelined. We're talking concussion, a broken limb, an ACL tear, a severely twisted ankle, deep cuts requiring stitches, etc. It means we've got to get you to a hospital, a clinic, a doctor. Being injured means you need treatment and time to heal in order to successfully recover.

A corporate lawyer friend of mine named Bruce reminded me recently that businesses experience those very same dilemmas every day.

"A company can go out of business or it can take a loss and press on," he said. "That's like being injured or hurt. The question for the people I work for is whether or not they can tell the difference, and whether or not they are properly positioned to change either outcome."

The way Bruce described it, if a company is injured, leadership can sometimes intervene to inspire and try to make it better—to take it from injured to hurt status. But if it is a sinking ship—say the bank is calling in the note—it may be time to end it. The challenge is in knowing the difference.

"If you just lost a deal to a competitor, it's only a wound. You are hurt, but you must and can keep pushing. Take it as a learning moment," he said. "If you can't pay the rent or employee salaries or the light bills on the warehouse, however, you might be really severely injured and need to throw in the towel."

Bruce made an analogy to automaker Toyota's troubles in 2009 and 2010. Toyota was forced to recall more than nine million cars and trucks after very public reports that several vehicles experienced unintended acceleration. More than fifty people reportedly died due to sticking pedals or incompatible floor mats, investigators later discovered. Both sales and production of Toyota vehicles were stopped briefly. Toyota later agreed to pay more than $1.2 billion in fines due to the scandal.

In 2011, floods, earthquakes, and tsunamis rocked Toyota's production efforts in Japan. Another recall for faulty power switch mechanics soon followed.

"A lot of people thought Toyota was going to get knocked out after those recalls," Bruce said. "But they proved they were just hurt, not irreparably injured. They fought their way out of it."

ABC News analysts reported in 2010 that "a combination of customer loyalty and uncharacteristically aggressive incentive offers have helped Toyota stay in the black despite the devastating hit it took to its reputation." This was in the wake of safety problems the company faced when Toyota vehicles seemingly accelerated uncontrollably.

Fortunately for the automaker, ABC said, its solid fiscal health meant it had money to spend on making the necessary repairs and on the sales incentive programs the company implemented.

David Lucas, the vice president of the research group Autodata, told the network, "If it had been a fragile company, [the recalls] certainly could have had a much larger impact."

In 2013, Bloomberg News reported that Toyota Motor Corporation outsold General Motors and Volkswagen AG to lead the global auto industry for the second straight year and forecast more than 10 million in sales for 2014 on rising demand in the United States and China.

Now, back to the two guys on my SEAL beach. Interestingly, after a little tough love and even less consolation, the guy who was hurt had tramped back into the frigid water and pushed through his pain; he couldn't have been more proud of himself two miles later. And the lion with the busted shoulder? By the time I saw him again, he'd already popped his shoulder back into place by himself, gotten cleared to continue training by an emergency room doctor, and gulped down a few anti-inflammatory pills to temper the pain. He wasn't about to give up on a commitment he'd made to his bad self. He continued to march and finished the course two days later with glory—albeit with some serious soreness. He had a broken body but not a busted spirit. At graduation, the others applauded his achievements.

The reality is, injuries are the price we pay for being SEALs. It's the same for anyone who's successful at anything.

The bottom line is this: If you're hurting or sore and you pull yourself out of the fight—whether it's physical or mental, a battlefield or a boardroom—you're making yourself a quitter. If you're truly *injured* and you have to leave the arena, you're someone who went down fighting.

Remember, being injured and being hurt are two distinctly different things. Never confuse the two. If you quit every time you feel pain, you'll never succeed at anything.

WHENEVER THERE IS DOUBT, THERE IS NO DOUBT

O NE OF THE MOST MOTIVATED and experienced former SEALs who works with me at SOT-G is a handsome lad named Geoff Reeves. Geoff is a model—now you understand the handsome crack—an actor, a luxury car racer and test driver, a master parachutist, and an action sports clothing line entrepreneur.

What matters most to me, however, is that Geoff is a tremendous leader of men. After earning an undergraduate degree in business pre-law from Bowling Green State University in 2000, Geoff attended Navy OCS (Officer Candidate School) and earned his commission as a Navy officer. He reported to BUD/S in 2001 and spent the next nine and a half years as a SEAL officer. Among his many accomplishments, Geoff helped commission SEAL Team Ten and served as its assistant officer in charge. After making Seal Team Ten's first deployment, Geoff was given command of the sixteen-man Navy Parachute Team, known as the "Leap Frogs." The "Frogs" perform dynamic parachute demonstrations into stadiums for Major League Baseball, National Football League, NASCAR, horse races, high schools, X Game events, etc., nationwide.

Geoff and I met on the set of the movie *Transformers* in 2007. He played a Secret Service agent in the film, and I acted as a military consultant. Ever since then, whenever I need a top-shelf instructor to help teach corporate clients the ways of SEAL leadership, Geoff is one of the first people I call.

In addition to be being incredible at tactics—I've personally seen him grab fear-frozen clients by their flak jackets during a CQB drill and heave them into rooms while screaming, "You're standing right in the middle of the kill zone, sir. Move it!!!"—Geoff is—no shocker here—also a remarkable strategic thinker.

I especially remember one time watching a seven-man boat crew of clients trying furiously to pass the surf zone in their rubber IBS boat. Getting the boat over fifteen-foot waves and past the break is an incredibly demanding and daunting task. The boat crews must time their attack and pick their target properly or risk getting slammed and tossed about like a cat in a washing machine. Success is all about proper timing and decision-making, as well as paddling like crazy.

One day, Geoff was evaluating a particular boat crew and the decisions they were making about whether or not to engage a particular wave. A fellow instructor voiced frustration with the team's seeming lack of initiative. "Why didn't they take that one? What's wrong with them?" the other instructor asked. Geoff shot a steely-eyed glance the guy's way and calmly said: "Whenever there is doubt, there is no doubt."

Less than twenty seconds later, the team attacked an eighteen-footer and was soon cresting the top, making it to the calm waters on the backside of the surf zone. They were the first of seven teams to summit the waves. Turns out, Geoff had given the same "no doubt" advice to his trainees as they marched out into the roaring surf. They had obviously listened to the master.

In some cases, doubt—or helpful hesitation—is a good thing. Like patience, it's not a pejorative. What Geoff was saying is that leaders have to feel *right* about something before they invest their precious time, hard-earned money, or lives in some effort. They have to *feel it* in their gut that it's the right call. Therefore, if something gives you pause or causes even the slightest doubt, the smart thing to do is to trust your intuition and instincts and act accordingly. If something smells fishy, it probably is. If it doesn't feel right, at the very least it may not be right for you. I'm not talking about being fearful of something. Fear is an emotion. I'm talking listening to your instinct and intuition. There's a difference.

Trusting your inner voice is not psychobabble. It's science. Author and anthropologist Helen Fisher says that the inner voice you hear is actually a form of unconscious reasoning—one that's rooted in the way our brains collect and store information. It's really learned expertise in disguise, she contends.

"As you accumulate knowledge—whether it's about what books your spouse likes or how to play chess—you begin to recognize patterns. Your brain unconsciously organizes these patterns into blocks of information—a process the late social scientist Herbert Simon, PhD, called *chunking*," Fisher says. "Over time your brain chunks and links more and more patterns, then stores these clusters of knowledge in your long-term memory. When you see a tiny detail of a familiar design, you instantly recognize the larger composition—and that's what we regard as a flash of intuition."

So when a shooter decides whether or not to take the shot, or an entrepreneur is faced with a decision whether or not to make a capital investment, partner with someone in a joint venture, or launch a new business, they are smart to trust their gut instincts. Does it feel . . . *right*? It's an essential first step in a smart decision-making process.

While no one uses the "there is no doubt" line with greater effect than Geoff, I'm pretty sure he cribbed it from the 1998 movie *Ronin*. In the film, Robert De Niro and Jean Reno play veteran Special Operations agents who are hired by a mysterious woman to track down a package that is wanted by both the Russians and the Irish. It's a great action flick. I highly recommend it, even if De Niro is former CIA and not a SEAL.

A *ronin,* by the way, was a samurai with no lord or master—a free-lancer between employers.

At one point in the movie, De Niro's character, Sam, thwarts an ambush of his team. Instead of going ahead with an arms exchange, he pulls the plug. It didn't feel right. The gutsy move saved his life and that of his team, as enemy snipers were lying in wait.

The following day, as Sam and his teammate Vincent, played by Reno, are sitting in a car during a stakeout, Vincent turns to Sam and asks:

VINCENT: *Under the bridge, by the river, how did you know it was an ambush?*

SAM: *Whenever there is any doubt, there is no doubt. That is the first thing they teach you.*

VINCENT: *Who taught you?*

SAM: *I don't remember. That's the second thing they teach you.*

In our case, feel free to remember Geoff as your teacher. And remember to trust your gut.

OPTIONS, ULTIMATUMS, AND VERSATILITY

ONE OF THE COVERT and clandestine ways that SEALs descend upon a target is by submarine. Nothing is as invisible and undetectable as a nuclear-powered fast-attack or missile sub hovering off the coast of some unsuspecting foreign country. And when necessary, nothing can better unleash America's lethal power than these unseen monsters of the deep. For SEALs, insertion by sub is as stealthy as it gets.

It's also a testament to our raison d'être: versatility.

Over the years, we have perfected our submarine insertion options. One of the most common—and unclassified—methods utilizes what we call a Dry Deck Shelter, or DDS, which is mounted onto the back of a submarine, behind the sail. In essence, the DDS is a thirty-eight-foot long, removable, spherical, submersible garage that holds SEAL toys, including our own minisubs known as Mark 8 Swimmer Delivery Vehicles, or SDVs, and our Combat Rubber Raiding Craft. Thanks to lockout trunks and multiple hyperbaric chambers, the DDS also allows us easy entrance to and exit from the submarine. (You can see videos of these assets on Navy-sponsored websites and YouTube channels. Just Google it.)

On many a mission, including during Operation Desert Storm, as well as on many a training exercise, I donned scuba gear and left the warm, dry confines of a submarine for the cold, dark ocean depths via a flooded DDS. Well below the ocean surface, my teammates and I would open the DDS's "garage doors" and remove our twenty-one-foot SDVs—either breathing from our own oxygen tanks or by using the vehicles' compressed-air supply. One SEAL would serve as the SDV pilot, another as copilot, and the rest of us made up the combat swimmer team. We all rode along on what we affectionately called "the sled."

Depending on how close the submarine can safely hover offshore, it can take hours for the SEAL teams to travel to their targets. Once there, we either conduct direct action or surveillance operations. When my teammates and I attacked Iraqi oil platforms during the Persian Gulf War, for example, it took hours for us and our SDV to make our way from the submarine to the target. But once there, we quietly anchored the SDV to the ocean bottom and swam to the platforms, making unannounced appearances that to the Iraqis must have seemed like we materialized via a *Star Trek*–like transporter. We later jumped back into the black water and, untethering the sled, drove it back to the waiting sub.

That kind of versatility is a huge force multiplier. SEALs never stop trying to adapt and innovate existing capabilities to tackle new and unseen challenges. For instance, the Navy continues to develop plans for next-generation underwater delivery systems that can improve the combat capability of SEAL forces. An Advanced SEAL Delivery System (ASDS) was built and launched in 2003 after years of study. It was designed to transport SEALs in a dry environment and leverage advanced sonar systems and unique electro-optical systems to give the SEALS improved undersea situational awareness. Unfortunately, the program was canceled due to cost overruns, but studies into other options continue.

For SEALs, such versatility is paramount. It's what makes us so special.

I've become convinced that in the business world, too, that kind of versatility is a cornerstone of competitiveness.

Our emblem, Neptune's Trident, stands for the versatility of the SEALs: we operate at Sea, in the Air, and on Land, and we proudly wear the trident on our chests.

As any leader will tell you, having options instead of ultimatums is a powerful position to be in. That's why when tasked with a mission, SEALs analyze multiple courses of action, or COAs as we call them. Sometimes in the mission planning process, the preferred COA is obvious. In that case we will recommend that a specific COA be taken. That said, providing options are where you make your money.

Let me give you a real life example. (I'm not divulging secrets here. In fact, I learned about these by reading reports widely publicized by news organizations and in books published by various individuals both in and out of government.) In Operation Neptune Spear, the raid to kill Osama bin Laden, the DEVGRU SEAL teams and their CIA partners developed at least four COAs to neutralize the target. Versatility was at the core of the COA set, which included:

1. The helicopter commando raid utilizing Black Hawk and Chinook helos and a team of hard-charging DEVGRU SEALs.

2. A B-2 Spirit stealth bomber attack. This COA involved plans for an obliterating air strike by the Air Force's massive, bat-wing-shaped strategic bombers, each of which can unload eighty 500-pound (230-kg) class Joint Direct Attack Munitions (JDAM) GPS-guided bombs with precision accuracy.

3. A joint operation with Pakistani forces.

4. A small but terribly effective laser-guided Small Tactical Munition (STM) fired from a drone as Osama tended to his garden.

The SEALs and the CIA developed these options based on the mission and versatility of our military forces. They soon analyzed—or war-gamed—each of the COAs, compared them to one another, and delivered the results and their recommendation to the president and his national security team.

In the end, despite initial misgivings by Vice President Joe Biden and Secretary of Defense Robert Gates, President Barack Obama chose the now-famous helicopter commando raid. His choice was based on myriad considerations, including possible civilian casualties, the need for unquestioned operational secrecy, and a political requirement that the United States could prove it was bin Laden who was killed. I believe President Obama made the tough and right call.

But Obama's decision was not made in a vacuum. He had multiple options to consider and evaluate. Plus he had a dynamically versatile team of SEALs to carry out his orders.

Those options and assets allowed President Obama to make the most forceful and, arguably, most fateful decision of his presidency.

Employees at all levels need to remember that providing options and versatility—not ultimatums—is what dynamic leaders require. And good leaders instill that mentality in their rank and file.

NO BETTER FRIEND—
NO WORSE ENEMY

IN 2013, one of the Marine Corps' most venerated and decorated leaders retired from active duty. His name was General James N. "Mad Dog" Mattis. And his moniker is more than appropriate. And like General Patton, General Mattis thinks like a Navy SEAL. He is the epitome of an engaged, decisive leader.

Mattis served the Corps for more than forty years, culminating in his final tour as leader of the US Central Command. CENTCOM forces have responsibility for the myriad Middle East hot spots that have kept America—and the world—so preoccupied for decades. It includes such volatile areas as Afghanistan, Iraq, Iran, Egypt, Pakistan, Yemen, and Saudi Arabia, to name a few. Needless to say, the warrior-statesman leadership responsibilities are immense.

At the time of his retirement, rumors were rampant that the Corps' four-star "Warrior Monk" was being forced out for asking Obama administration officials too many pesky, pointed questions about America's plans and policies regarding Iran. (His reputation for speaking truth to power was legendary.) It was clear to all, however, that even when Mattis spouted off, in the end he'd always salute smartly and carry out his orders—whatever the risk and danger.

When the good general left the ranks, rank-and-file Marines

were understandably devastated. That's because over the course of his career, Mattis honed a well-deserved reputation as both a ruthless and aggressive battlefield commander and a beloved leader who respected and cared more about "his marines" than he did himself. He was a lead-from-the-front, warrior-scholar kind of guy who inspired his troops, infuriated his bosses, and terrified America's enemies.

Albert C. Pierce, the director of the Institute for National Security Ethics and Leadership at the National Defense University, once introduced Mattis to an audience by telling the following story:

A couple of months ago, when I told General [Charles C.] Krulak, the former Commandant of the Marine Corps, now the chair of the Naval Academy Board of Visitors, that we were having General Mattis speak this evening, he said, "Let me tell you a Jim Mattis story." When General Krulak was Commandant of the Marine Corps, every year, starting about a week before Christmas, he and his wife would bake hundreds and hundreds and hundreds of Christmas cookies. They would package them in small bundles.

Then on Christmas day, he would load his vehicle. At about 4 a.m., General Krulak would drive himself to every Marine guard post in the Washington-Annapolis-Baltimore area and deliver a small package of Christmas cookies to whatever Marines were pulling guard duty that day. He said that one year, he had gone down to Quantico as one of his stops to deliver Christmas cookies to the Marines on guard duty. He went to the command center and gave a package to the lance corporal who was on duty.

"I asked, 'Who's the officer of the day?' The lance corporal said, 'Sir, it's Brigadier General Mattis.' And I said, 'No, no, no. I know who General Mattis is. I mean, who's the officer of the day today, Christmas Day?' The lance corporal, feeling a little anxious, said, 'Sir, it is Brigadier General Mattis.'

"About that time, I spotted in the back room a cot, or a day-bed. I said, 'No, Lance Corporal. Who slept in that bed last night?' The lance corporal said, 'Sir, it was Brigadier General Mattis.'

"About that time, General Mattis came in, in a duty uniform with a sword. I said, 'Jim, what are you doing here on Christmas Day? Why do you have duty?'" General Mattis told Krulak that the young officer who was scheduled to have duty on Christmas Day had a family, and General Mattis decided it was better for the young officer to spend Christmas Day with his family, and so he chose to have duty on Christmas Day.

That's the kind of officer that Jim Mattis is.

General Mattis also had a penchant for blunt talk. The following are ten of his most notable—and inspiring—quotes, as reported and compiled by various war correspondents and media outlets, including the *San Diego Union-Tribune* and the *Business Insider*. In these words, delivered to his marines, his congressional overseers, and even his adversaries over the years, Mattis conveys some essential truths about vigilance, discipline, professionalism, innovation, adaptation, lifelong learning, and leadership. They certainly motivate the hell out of me. Enjoy.

1. "I come in peace. I didn't bring artillery. But I'm pleading with you, with tears in my eyes: If you fuck with me, I'll kill you all."

2. "There are hunters and there are victims. By your discipline, you will decide if you are a hunter or a victim."

3. "We've backed off in good faith to try and give you a chance to straighten this problem out. But I am going to beg with you

for a minute. I'm going to plead with you, do not cross us. Because if you do, the survivors will write about what we do here for ten thousand years."

4. "If in order to kill the enemy you have to kill an innocent, don't take the shot. Don't create more enemies than you take out by some immoral act."

5. "I don't lose any sleep at night over the potential for failure. I cannot even spell the word."

6. "The most important six inches on the battlefield is between your ears."

7. "In this age, I don't care how tactically or operationally brilliant you are, if you cannot create harmony—even vicious harmony—on the battlefield based on trust across service lines, across coalition and national lines, and across civilian/ military lines, you need to go home, because your leadership is obsolete. We have got to have officers who can create harmony across all those lines."

8. "A country that armed Stalin to defeat Hitler can certainly work alongside enemies of al-Qaida to defeat al-Qaida."

9. "You are part of the world's most feared and trusted force. Engage your brain before you engage your weapon."

10. "Demonstrate to the world there is 'No Better Friend, No Worse Enemy' than a US Marine."

HUMILITY

IT'S AMAZING what you can accomplish if you don't care who gets the credit.

I'm not the first person to utter that phrase, but you'd be hard-pressed to find anyone who believes it more deeply.

When SEAL teams are operating at optimal levels, it's all about the mission—not the accomplishments or egos of any individual team members. There's a word for such behavior: humility.

When teams rally around a mission—whether it's to snatch and grab some bad guy in some far-flung country or prep the boss for the annual stockholders meeting—and put the mission before self, the probabilities for success are staggering. Obstacles are more easily surmounted, problems are circumnavigated, and efficiencies are increased when high-performing individuals commit to one clear goal: mission success. Rank and ego be damned. It's a beautiful thing to behold. It's also quite rare.

In today's hypercompetitive, self-absorbed world full of divas raised on a culture of self-promotion and oversharing (Facebook!), having a healthy sense of humility is a complete anathema to many people. Yet humility is the bedrock of any high-speed team. It's also a requirement to be a Navy SEAL.

You've no doubt noticed precious few operational details of my many SEAL adventures in this book. That's by design. SEALs don't tolerate braggarts or glory hounds, the "look-at-me" types who constantly crave attention, adulation, and individual accolades. Those guys usually wash out early in training after it becomes dazzlingly clear that they are simply in it for themselves. They are the sorts who want a trident just so they can wear it on their uniform and say they are a Navy SEAL. Those sorts of personalities—the one-wayers, as I call them—will ultimately undermine unit cohesion and jeopardize our chances at mission success if we let them on the bus. Plus, they are annoying as hell.

Instead, successful SEALs are proud to be known as quiet professionals. Most Special Forces operators adhere to the same code. We fly under the radar. We're focused, mature, and even-handed individuals. We're also painstakingly discreet. In addition to enhancing unit cohesion, humility and discretion also ensure operational security. For us, that's a no-brainer. It we don't have operational security, missions can go haywire and people get killed.

It's imperative that leaders instill a culture of humility, teamwork, and mission focus within an organization. And that starts at the top. The best leaders, for example, should be the ones giving credit, not taking it. Sharing credit shows you are a team player, that you're more interested in the team than yourself.

"When one of my floor managers says 'the project's' success is thanks to John over on the production line, and John says the real reason for the success 'is because Joe over in manufacturing' made something happen, and Joe says 'thanks for the thought, but it was really Susie in accounting who deserves the bulk of the credit' . . . I know I've got an amazing team and an incredible corporate culture," said James, a client who runs a tool-making enterprise.

Being humble is a freeing mentality for those confident enough to fully embrace it, actually. I know lots of hotshots who spend their entire careers scratching and clawing their way to career stagnation because they believe the path to success lies in undermining others and endless self-promotion. They are constantly scheming and devising ways to cut the legs out from under someone else. Talk about a waste of mental energy. All they do is end up ticking off their more humble bosses and alienating their colleagues. (Notice I didn't say teammates. These guys don't see coworkers as teammates but, rather, as competitors.) Even when they do something special, their obsessive ambition tarnishes any achievement. Instead of focusing on the mission of the company—and figuring out where they can best fit in and serve the collective team effort—they are instead that guy sitting at the conference table incessantly raising his hand with a frantic "look at me" expression. At the same time, they condescendingly dismiss the ideas of others. They sulk and pout if they are not looked upon— or repeatedly acknowledged—as the smartest guy in the room. And they wonder why they never get the promotion or recognition they believe they deserve.

S. Gary Snodgrass, an executive vice president and chief human resources officer at Exelon, an energy company in Chicago, once told the *New York Times* that even if you accomplish something exemplary, you never "want to alienate anyone by promoting it too aggressively." "Focus on 'we,' not 'me,'" Snodgrass told the *Times*. "Individuals will have a better chance of receiving kudos for their work if they put their egos on the shelf and emphasize how the outcome was the result of a team effort."

Funny how that works. I honestly believe good things happen to good people.

SEALs know that our power comes from the team, not from the individuals who comprise it. We also take great pride in being part of something bigger than ourselves—our team and our mission. We don't need parades or public pronouncements to feel good about ourselves or our work. Our work speaks for itself—at least the work that leaks out in the press now and again.

No, we're happiest when we're among ourselves, behind closed doors, handing out awards that others—save our teammates—will never see for missions they will never know about. That's the power of the team.

We know we're badasses, and we know the country knows it, too. We don't need to crow about it. Enough said.

HAVE A MISSION
COMMAND MENTALITY

SEAL TEAMS THRIVE when operating on the edge. That's the place our enemies least expect us. It's also where the most opportunity awaits. When a small, decentralized team is properly staffed, trained, and trusted it can operate on the edge—and any precarious ledge—with devastating alacrity.

Commanders depend upon a SEAL team's disciplined initiative and aggressive, independent actions in pursuit of mission success. We routinely deliver on those expectations because each team member possesses the mental agility to frame and reframe problems quickly. Each of us can also be counted on to carry out the Commander's Intent. We're a force in constant readiness that trains as hard as it fights.

As a result, our commanders trust us enough to make the key calls when things go kinetic (crazy). We don't have to ask permission, and we just might violate earlier guidance or orders if it makes sense to us to do so.

Pushing that decision-making power down to the team level is what fuels the SEAL team's effectiveness and ability to act. It's what empowers us to operate successfully on the edge.

Are your teams similarly equipped and organized? Do you trust them to do what you intend? Are you willing to let go?

Not every leader is willing to relinquish the requisite control to empower a dynamic, decentralized team. Or they are unable to articulate and deliver the sort of "mission-type" orders that provide both intent and parameters that allow the team to effectively maneuver in their "battle" space. I witness these behaviors a lot as I coach my corporate clients. I try to help them realize that nervous leaders who micromanage fail to empower their teams—thereby failing to do what elite military units do: promote a culture that values risk as a means to generate opportunity.

The Navy's sister service, the Marines, coined a terrific phrase for this mindset back in the mid-1990s. General Charles C. Krulak, whom we met earlier and who served as commandant of the Corps from 1995 to 1999, famously referred to the "strategic corporal" when he discussed Marine Corps unit operations in places like Haiti, Somalia, and Bosnia.

In an increasingly uncertain and complex world, Krulak believed, the Corps had to willingly entrust its lowest-ranking noncommissioned officers and team leaders—the corporals—with the tactical independence and decision-making authority that could have worldwide strategic implications—both positive or negative. It was a hard but necessary sell.

"The clear lesson of our past is that success in combat, and in the barracks for that matter, rests with our most junior leaders," Krulak wrote in *Marines* magazine at the time. "Over the years, however, a perception has grown that the authority of our NCO's has been eroded. Some believe that we have slowly stripped from them the latitude, the discretion, and the authority necessary to do their job. That perception must be stamped out. The remaining vestiges of the 'zero defects mentality' must be exchanged for an environment in which all Marines are afforded the 'freedom to fail' and with it, the *opportunity to succeed*. Micro-management must become a thing of the past and supervision—that double-edged sword—must be complemented by proactive mentoring. Most importantly, we must aggressively *empower* our NCO's, hold them strictly accountable for their actions, and allow the leadership potential within each of them to flourish."

In short, Krulak wanted a return to the sort of small-unit teamwork and leadership that helped write the legacy of the Corps and win such battles as Iwo Jima and Belleau Wood.

But while the general was spot-on, the notion of the need for what's known today as "Mission Command" (decentralization, rapid [and lower-level] decision-making, and units operating in autonomous environments) is not new. SEALs have been doing it since we were created as a fighting unit. Older still, the German armed forces have been embracing it since the time of Frederick the Great. They call the revolutionary command philosophy *Auftragstaktikt,* and it served as the tactical backbone of the Wehrmacht in World War II: less paperwork and doctrine, fewer detailed orders, and trust in a well-trained, well-equipped team led by fiery-eyed men and women of competence and character.

This sort of command culture is thankfully ingrained in the SEAL training and education pipeline, but less so in the larger, more hidebound US military. That's part of what makes SEALs so unique. We disdain doctrine and instead promote teams made up of adaptive, agile, free, and independent thinkers.

I've seen how such philosophy permeates some dynamic corporations. I've also seen it completely absent in others where rigid, inflexible command structures regularly create disaster.

Writing in the *Harvard Business Review* in 2010, former marine and author Rye Barcott sang the praises and possibilities of *Auftragstaktikt* on both the battlefield and the boardroom.

When he was a twenty-two-year-old lieutenant, "we were being trained to obey orders, but also to make them. We were being trained to think, to be teachers as well as students and soldiers," Barcott wrote. "As young lieutenants, we learned that we needed to set the example, communicate the commander's intent, and then empower our corporals and sergeants to operate in places where they may not be able to ask, 'What do I do next?'"

That training helped Barcott as he infiltrated the business world. Like me, Barcott believes that today's businesses need thinkers and doers. In his words: "They need strategic corporals."

"It's been four years since I left the active duty for a three-year graduate school program in business management and public administration. Now in my first full-time job in the private sector as a commercial associate at Duke Energy, I am struck by the level of uncertainty in business, even in a regulated utility, which is among the most stable of enterprises," Barcott wrote. "In conditions of constant uncertainty and change, there is tremendous need for leaders and project managers who take the initiative to identify solutions to problems in their earliest stages, and have the execution skills to follow through, mobilize others, and complete tasks."

Amen, my brother.

So, how do you instill such a culture in your workplace? First, you hire the sorts of people who reflect your ethos and values. You ensure they have the proper education and an infinitely agile mindset. Then you thoroughly train them and outfit them with the finest equipment you possibly can. You trust them to make the right decisions. You push them to the edge.

And then, on your command, you unleash them. And meet them later on the high ground.

EMBRACE THE SUCK

SEALS ARE MASTERS at embracing the suck.

That is to say, if the going gets bad, you suck it up. You may not like it, whatever it is, but it's essential that you lead your way through it.

If you can embrace the suck, you can overcome almost any obstacle or difficulty. And one of the best ways to do that is with humor.

The Spartan warrior Dienekes knew all about embracing the suck. Herodotus, the famous Greek historian, wrote that on the eve of the Battle of Thermopylae, Dienekes was told that the Persian army was so numerous that their archers would block out the sun with their arrows. Dienekes reportedly laughed heartily and offered this suck-embracing reply: "Good, then we shall have our battle in the shade!"

Fast-forward two thousand years. When the Marines found themselves surrounded by Chinese troops near the "Frozen Chosin" Reservoir during the Korean War, Colonel Lewis "Chesty" Puller reportedly told his men: "We've been looking for the enemy for some time now. We've finally found him. We're surrounded. That simplifies things."

You get the point. When a leader is forced to dine on a crap sandwich, it's better they meet it head-on with a smile, than by cowering in fear and trepidation. Trust me: the people who are counting on you will positively respond to your confidence and composure.

When I was in BUD/S and on the Teams, one of the motivational phrases I always used when things went sour was "Well, at least it's not raining." In essence, things could always be worse. Covered in sand, exhausted from running for miles on end, and freezing your ass off in the pounding surf? "At least it's not raining." Extract helo late in arriving, leaving you hunkering down in the tree line behind enemy lines? "At least it's not raining."

Don't be confused. This isn't about being a wise guy. Humor, in these cases, is more than just bravado, wisecracking, or machismo. It's about motivation, inspiration, and hope. It's about leadership.

Remember, enjoy the shade. And be thankful when you're surrounded. Now you can you shoot in all directions!

YOU'VE GOT TO
CARE ABOUT THOSE
YOU LEAD

U NLESS YOU TRULY, deeply, and genuinely care about the
people you lead, you will never form an elite team. Nor will
you ever be considered an effective leader. Unfortunately, too many
leaders are disengaged from the people they are in charge of, are dis-
ingenuous in their dealings with them, or are downright negative in
their actions. Stranger still is the fact that the act of truly caring for
someone is one of the easiest things a leader can do. And it reaps staggering benefits for both individuals and organizations.

For SEAL team leaders, while the mission may come first, the
people—the team—is what's most important. We recognize that people are more important than hardware. Without our people, there's
no mission to tackle or anything to lead. It doesn't mean we are all
close friends. In fact, I've served with guys about whom I honestly
had no idea whether or not they were married, had kids, or even had a
girlfriend. But it doesn't mean that I didn't care deeply about them as
individuals or do everything I could to ensure their well-being. I did.
And they knew it. And the feeling was reciprocated.

Caring means giving of your time and energy to others, to talk to and—more important—to listen to them. It means understanding their values and attitudes, and alleviating their needs—whether physical or emotional. It means teaching, training, and coaching. It means doing what you can to develop them as operators, and ensuring they have what they need to get their job done. It means providing a safe and healthy workplace where everyone is respected and discrimination or harassment is not tolerated. It means creating and following policies and procedures that are designed to help others succeed. For SEALs, it means adhering to the sacred obligation to ensure everyone is properly trained to survive on the battlefield. It means establishing standards of performance and then demanding they be implemented and adhered to. It means not putting yourself above others. It means if there are not enough cots for everyone to sleep on, then everyone—including the commanding general—sleeps on the ground. It means being fair and honest—and letting others know how you feel, whether it's good or bad. It means getting out of the office and down on the production floor and genuinely appreciating the efforts and sacrifices people make on your behalf.

It's about respect.

I once read a pointed list of characteristics of the uncaring leader. An Army War College student had compiled it while researching a paper on historic examples of the caring military leader. The "Lessons Learned" are apropos to every organization, I believe: Uncaring leaders waste people's time and skills. They don't hold others accountable. They don't inform their people and, even worse, they ignore them. They don't notice or mind that their troops are ill-prepared or untrained. They lack basic human understanding and compassion. They consider people expendable.

I always find it amazing when people look at me quizzically after I tell them that caring for others is one of the fundamental principles of good leadership. I watch their faces droop when I tell them that the ten thousand dollars they spent on the corporate picnic last year to "thank" their employees was less effective for employee morale than if they simply gave someone a genuine smile and a handshake on the shop floor.

Writing in *Forbes* magazine, businessman John Hall said that employees who feel valued and appreciated by their leaders are infinitely more likely to go above and beyond for the company and hold themselves accountable for their part of a project.

"Most important, they will be happier in their roles," he said. "If leaders disregard the importance of connecting with employees, they lose the benefit of a dedicated, long-term team."

Hall suggests that leaders try harder to personally help their employees and to make efforts to relate to them and not to act like they are above them. He recommends that you show you care about their personal lives and show an interest in their significant others. Other ways to show appreciation: Create new experiences for your employees. And simply make time for them.

When you honestly care about the well-being of your employees, you'll be amazed at what they'll do for and with you. When you're in it together, the possibilities are endless.

YOU CAN ONLY
MANAGE WHAT YOU
CAN MEASURE

O NE OF THE best things about being at the tip of the spear is that you get the best toys. SEALs and other Special Operations forces routinely receive the latest technologically advanced gear, despite whatever "fiscal austerity" measures Uncle Sam might face.

And when you pair advanced technology with highly motivated, highly trained warriors, the chances for mission success are exponentially improved.

Technology improves a SEAL's ability not only to be more effective, but to defeat the enemy even before any shots are fired. It provides us with essential situational awareness, or SA, which streamlines and informs the decision-making process. It delivers battlefield intelligence, the sorts of information that puts us one or more steps ahead of the bad guys. It helps untangle a complicated maneuver space, allowing us to operate with freedom and confidence and to strike at the time and place of our choosing.

The acquisition and application of advanced technology is a core requirement for our business. And the best business leaders I counsel feel the same way about their line of work. Many of them adhere to the business maxim that it's easier to manage what you can measure. To that end—and while we know full well that not all things are truly measurable—technology is one sure way to better measure facts and variables. Staying ahead of the curve is a continual—but necessary—commitment.

While the rest of the world continues to be amazed by unmanned aerial reconnaissance vehicles—platforms like the well-known Predator and the Reaper hunter/killer/intelligence collector drones that have devastated al-Qaida to great effect over the past decade—the SEALs consider them yesterday's news. Today, SEAL teams deploy hand-launched UAVs, such as the 4.2-pound Raven, or the Lockheed RQ-170 Sentinel—known as the Beast of Kandahar. We use beer-can-sized "throwbots"—pint-sized robots with infrared cameras and wireless transmitters—to help take down buildings. SEALs are armed with facial recognition software and retina scanners to help separate the good guys from the bad; we are delivered to hot spots in customized Black Hawk helos or in CV-22 tilt-rotor Ospreys where we roar out of the plane's belly in souped-up all-terrain vehicles equipped with the most advanced weapons and navigation systems imaginable. We wear night-vision equipment that's so advanced, it's considered a national secret. And we get the latest guns and ammunition available anywhere.

Among the best-kept secrets of the US military are the projects developed by the Defense Advanced Research Projects Agency (DARPA), which was established in 1958. SEALs love this joint. Its goal: "to prevent strategic surprise from negatively impacting U.S. national security and create strategic surprise for U.S. adversaries by maintaining the technological superiority of the U.S. military."

This amazing agency "advances knowledge through basic research" and "creates innovative technologies that address current practical problems through applied research." This is where ideas like wearable superstrength exoskeletons are tried and tested and small, four-man helicopters are tested. Where laser blasters are a reality. DARPA conducts everything from laboratory experiments to creating full-scale technology demonstrations in such diverse fields as biology, medicine, computer science, chemistry, physics, engineering, mathematics, material sciences, social sciences, and neuroscience.

DARPA is known as the Defense Department's primary innovation engine. Better still, they help create lasting, revolutionary change and both create and prevent strategic surprise.

It's not an option for a successful business leader to not know and use the latest technology. It's your competitive weapon.

Technology is at the very heart of one of my favorite sports stores—Jack Rabbit, in New York City. Whenever I need a new pair of running shoes I head to Jack Rabbit because of the high-tech treadmill analysis they use to determine my foot strike while running. And they do it right there in the store. Jack Rabbit was one of the first sports stores to leverage technology to enhance their credibility and authority in their market while at the same time providing a valuable and unique service to customers. By having me run on a treadmill equipped with cameras and sensors to record impact data, the store salespeople can authoritatively recommend the best shoe for me. And I am part of the process. It's empowering and serves to create a high degree of confidence in my purchase decision.

Technology provides advantage. Advantage enables success. The successful leader must stay ahead of the technological curve. If you don't, your competitor certainly will.

THE BELL

A SEAL IS NOTHING if not resilient. Our ability to thrive and persevere—both mentally and physically—in any situation is legendary. We're indefatigable.

But let me let you in on a secret. SEALs are a special breed because individual men *decided* they wanted to be that way. It's not like they have special gifts that others don't have. It isn't bestowed by some maniacal BUD/S instructor. It doesn't come from training or education. There are no pills or potions, either. Rather, these men made conscious choices to leave the "average" behind. They reached down deep into their souls and found something few others ever discover: a can-do, booyah mindset that's devoted to doing what it takes—whatever it takes—in order to get the job done.

They committed themselves fully—to themselves, to a cause, and to their team.

The harsh, physical demands of Navy SEAL training were created by design. As I've made clear from the start, BUD/S is a kick in the nuts. The only way to survive it—to defeat it—is to commit to doing so, whatever the consequences. There are no off-ramps, no bypasses. For the truly committed, no amount of pain, cold, wet, and tired can derail their devotion to the cause. But halfhearted commitments are exposed early and often. As are the truly dedicated. I've seen kids—and clients—literally crawling on all fours in the sand—frothing at the mouth, bleeding from the elbows, oblivious to the howls of others around them—making a desperate, dedicated plunge to the finish line. Those are the sorts of guys I want on my team. Guys who finish what they started, give it everything they have, and only quit when they have passed out or passed the finish line.

At the same time, I've seen many a man convince himself into believing his legs can't take one . . . more . . . step; can't stand the cold for even one . . . more . . . second. Those are the guys I pity; those are the guys I don't want on my team. Don't get me wrong, it doesn't make them bad people. It just means they don't have what it takes, mentally and physically.

At BUD/S and at SOT-G, there's one iconic symbol for what separates the warriors from the weak. The Bell. It's a traditional shiny brass ship's bell affixed to a pole and positioned for all to see. I keep ours anchored in front of our headquarters tent, a place known as the drop area. If at any time someone wants a one-way ticket out of training, all they have to do is walk up to the Bell, ring it three times, and it's "Hasta la vista, baby."

For the quitters, it's the fastest and cheapest one-way ticket back to Average Town. And man, at times it's alluring. Ringing the Bell means a hot shower and a warm bed, good food, and an end to the torture of training. It means no more sand in every one of your bodily cavities, no more screaming instructors, no more fear, no more pain. But as I tell my clients—it also means no glory.

Like BUD/S, life is going to hurl things your way that sometimes seem unimaginable. Whether it's a personal financial disaster, a failed relationship, a stalled career, a medical emergency, or an existential threat to your business—you have two choices: finish the race to the very best of your ability, or ring the Bell. You're either committed or you're quitting.

Winners tell the little naysaying voice in their heads to shut up.

They know that the chances are good that all the pain and suffering they're enduring now will seem funny someday down the line. They'll look back on the challenges and take pride in the fact that they finished what they started, that they honestly tested and pushed themselves to the limits of their ability, that they mastered something that most people will never master. Winners remember why they were there in the first place, and later bask in the glory of having done it.

I recently read a blog post on the online professional network LinkedIn (yes, I'm also a member!). The post noted several very famous business leaders who were once down, but never out. The list was quite impressive:

"Henry Ford—the pioneer of modern business entrepreneurs and the founder of the Ford Motor Company failed a number of times on his route to success. His first venture to build a motor car got dissolved a year and a half after it was started because the stockholders lost confidence in him. Ford was able to gather enough capital to start again but a year later pressure from his financiers forced him out of the company again. Despite the fact that the entire motor industry had lost faith in him, he managed to find another investor to start the Ford Motor Company—and the rest is history.

"Walt Disney—one of the greatest visionaries of all time who created the global Disney empire of film studios, theme parks and consumer products didn't start off as a success. Believe it or not, Walt was fired from an early job at the *Kansas City Star* newspaper because he was not creative enough! In 1922 he started his first company called Laugh-O-Gram. The Kansas-based business produced cartoons and short advertising films. In 1923, the business went bankrupt. Walt didn't give up, he packed up, went to Hollywood and started The Walt Disney Company.

"Richard Branson—founder of Virgin Atlantic, Virgin Music and Virgin Active. When he was 16 he dropped out of school to start a student magazine that didn't do as well as he hoped. He then set up a mail-order record business which did so well that he opened his own record shop called Virgin. Along the road to ultimate success came many other failed ventures, including Virgin Cola, Virgin Vodka, Virgin Clothes, Virgin Vie, Virgin cards, etc."

Take solace in knowing that legendary entrepreneurs like Branson, Ford, and Disney were once down, but they were never out. Remember, if you ring the Bell, it will resonate in your head for a lifetime. You'll take that demon with you to the grave. I'd rather be a loser than a quitter anytime.

I've been a lifelong fan of the on-field spirit of baseball all-time hit leader Pete Rose. His personal struggles with gambling aside, the switch-hitting legend is known as much for his spirit as his skills. Where other players had more natural talent, Rose made up the difference through the sheer force of will and determination. He committed himself fully to his craft, even when it didn't come naturally. He deserved his "Charlie Hustle" nickname. He ran out walks, slid head-first into bases, and did whatever it took to win. He worked harder than other people, and he never quit.

"People say I don't have great tools. They say that I can't throw like Ellis Valentine or run like Tim Raines or hit with power like Mike Schmidt," Rose once said. "Who can? I make up for it in other ways, by putting out a little bit more. That's my theory, to go through life hustling."

If you want to win, you've got to hustle. Remember, you can sleep when you're dead. Pain is good. And extreme pain . . . *very* good.

Here's what some of the executives who took the course had to say:

Yacov Wrocherinsky *is founder and CEO of Infinity Info Systems, a New York City–based information technology consulting firm focused on customer relationship management (CRM) and business analytics solutions for clients in the financial, life sciences, business services, media, and manufacturing/distribution industries around the world.*

The recent economic crisis affected all businesses in one way or another. As business owners, it is our duty and our responsibility to lead our organizations through these difficult times. Recently a group of entrepreneurs and I were fortunate to learn some lessons in corporate leadership from a rather unconventional source, a group of former Navy SEALs. What I learned during a four-day boot camp with the Young Presidents' Organization's YPO/U.S. Navy SEALs Challenge in October 2008 also can help you and your organization through these difficult times.

TRAINING IS VITAL: During the program the physical training, which included ocean swimming, carrying heavy logs, pull-ups for food, and sleep deprivation, was designed to push our mental and physical limits as well as teach us to work as a team. Constant training is an essential reason why the Navy SEALs are always ready to perform any mission, and should be part of the culture of all businesses. The company that is not learning is not growing. You should constantly challenge yourself to improve your organization.

DEFINE YOUR MISSION: For the SEALs, defining the mission and objective is critical to the success of the team. In business, sometimes the big goal may seem too great to achieve; for example, a company with revenues of $5 million wants to grow to $10 million in two years. Some of the missions we executed in our training seemed equally as daunting. To make it easier, we identified the big objectives, broke them down into incremental goals, and then into individual tasks. Success became a function of everyone completing individual tasks within the structure of the team.

GATHER INTELLIGENCE: Information is the most powerful weapon and tool for success. After defining our mission, we then gathered as much intelligence as we could on the target, its surroundings, threats, opportunities, and possible contingencies. Intelligence is as vital to the success of a military mission as it is to the success of your business. When you know what is going on with your company, customers, employees, competition, and your marketplace, you can identify opportunities, open up new ideas, and formulate a proper plan for success.

PLAN, PLAN, PLAN: Planning is vital. This is putting the intelligence you gathered into practical application and thinking through contingencies and obstacles. During our training, we had to plan each mission, but sometimes only had a few minutes to do so. With the current economic crisis, businesses also don't have the luxury of time and need to assess their situations quickly and put plans in place to move forward. Plans provide solid instructions on how you will reach your objectives. Without a plan, employees lack direction and can become frustrated and uninspired. Just as the SEALs come together to complete a mission, your organization will work together to reach its goals, if you have a plan.

EMBRACE AND ADAPT TO CHANGE: In war—as in life—the only constant is change. During our missions the instructors constantly altered situations and threw obstacles in our way. We quickly learned to assess the situation, formulate a strategy, communicate to our team, and execute the new plan. In business, change can derail your team. As the leader you have to teach your team to understand that change is inevitable and provide them a process to handle it. By doing so you will create a strong, adaptable organization that will meet its objectives no matter what happens in the market.

ANSWERING THE CALL: During the presidential election we often heard about the dreaded "two a.m. phone call" and which candidate could be trusted to answer it. Businesses got their call in September [2008] with the collapse of the credit market. As leaders, we have no choice but to answer it. When I was roused from my bunk by my instructors at 2 a.m. for the first of many grueling, cold water conditioning sessions in the 60-degree ocean, I was disoriented, confused, and barely alert, much like many of you feel today; afraid to act and unsure of what to do. I learned a game plan, a template to deal with any situation and overcome it. Today many of us are in a battle for the very survival of our businesses. Just as the SEALs accomplish the impossible missions, you can succeed by adopting these principles in your business. And while failure is not an option for a SEAL, it is also not an option for us as business leaders today.

Ross Bushman is president and CEO of Cast-Fab Technologies, a combined metal casting foundry and fabrication job shop located in Cincinnati, Ohio, that employs 280 people and has annual sales in excess of $50 million.

I am a married, forty-three-year-old father of two. My wife pushed me to sign up for the YPO Leadership Under Fire program given my admiration of the SEALs and her desire to get me off "couch potato" status. I have a bad back that went downhill several years ago. While I had been trying to "work out" now and then, I didn't have a goal and it was difficult to make real progress. I had to be one of the people in my LUF class who had to come the farthest in terms of physically getting ready for the program. (Not something to brag about, but a reality.)

My business, Cast-Fab Technologies, operates in a tough environment. We run a foundry and fabrication facility. We pour molten iron into sand molds for large castings up to 80,000 pounds. We make parts for the mining, machine tool, oil and gas, and the defense industries. It can be unbearably hot in the summer and tough during the winter months as well. I was looking for a personal challenge, but also a way to apply some military teamwork and discipline techniques to my organization. The SEALs and their "unit integrity" mindset seemed like a perfect fit.

I knew the LUF program would be physically the toughest thing I had done in my life, but I was surprised by the level of the mental challenge involved. While I expected to have to play games in my head to push through, the instructors did a great job of purposely playing some mind games to make us uncomfortable and to keep us guessing.

It is easy to foster great teamwork when you are at an off-site training program, or after your company receives a big contract. The key is to keep it together under adversity. While we don't have bullets flying at us, we do have sparks and molten iron to contend with every day. Tempers can get short and trust gets tested. I have several takeaways from the LUF program. One of the most important ones is that the team must stay together to finish together. You don't get points for having one or two teammates arrive at the finish line first. If an area is struggling, everyone better be lending a hand.

I will also say that after having completed the LUF program and accomplishing several tasks that I thought were almost impossible, the day-to-day issues at work don't seem so insurmountable anymore.

*S*alomon Sacal *is CEO of Ascenda Corporation, an international business consultancy and purchasing outsourcing firm that operates in the Pacific Rim, Asia, North America, Latin America, and Europe.*

The most important thing I learned from Rob and his team of Navy SEALs is the enduring value of planning, adaptability, and perseverance.

I know how critical it is to constantly adapt to different cultures and situations in order to be successful. Rob certainly reinforced that mentality. When a successful entrepreneur realizes that the way things are being done in a certain sector isn't working, he sees an opportunity. But one must act decisively, too. When you pair such vision with nimble adaptability, a spark is created that often results in a lucrative new business or project.

The most important part of starting a new business is always the beginning. That's because there are numerous uncertainties and questions. Proper strategic planning is key to survival. Just like the hundreds of SEAL candidates at BUD/S training who never earn their tridents, while there are many new start-ups, there are few that actually become successful businesses. At the beginning a business can very easily fail due to lack of human resources, cash-flow, and initial sales, to name but a few factors. But you can't give up. Detailed planning, execution, and persistence are critical to getting you off the ground.

For the entrepreneur, just as for the SEALs, quitting is never an option. That mantra has helped me to view the hard times I experience at the beginning of a start-up as training for what will be required for future success. Still, one must also be pragmatic. If a business folds at the start-up stage, for example, it's usually better than folding further on down the road where it will cause more damage to everyone involved. That's not quitting. That's being prudent and responsible.

But all entrepreneurs must be prepared to weather the dark moments. The only way to do that is to keep pushing. As Rob likes to say, "The only way out is through." You must prepare to face the many challenges that lie ahead at the start of the new venture. Some drawbacks are inevitable. So prepare yourself, your team, and your executive-level management for these inevitabilities.

Once you make it through the start-up stage—like SEALs in training—the likelihood of success is greater, as long as you keep planning, adapting, and persevering in new and changing environments. I still hear Rob saying that "pain is temporary, but quitting will last forever." Very true. I am confident that my new business venture will succeed as long as my team and I use the strategic lessons Rob has taught me, focusing on our goal, and getting there—as a team—together.

Gregg Snyder, thirty-seven, Houston, Texas

I was a corporate banker for ten years; I always wanted to take the chance at owning a business. I knew the risks were high but so are the rewards. Presently, my brother and I have a private equity investment platform and invest in many types of businesses—oil and gas production and midstream, industrial shipyard, boiler and heat exchange repair, and an employment agency.

I completed LUF in September 2013. I was enrolled in the previous-year LUF but did not attend due to a dislocated shoulder. I worked hard for a year to prepare myself both mentally and physically for LUF the following year.

On the first night, during the second night swim evolution, my shoulder dislocated and I knew that I was going to need to go to the hospital to have my shoulder put back into place. After a 1.5-mile walk in great pain with my shoulder hanging out I managed to put my shoulder back into the socket. I knew I could have easily dropped out of the program given my medical condition. But I did not. Instead, I decided I simply had to "adjust for the pain," as our instructors kept saying.

In life, business, combat, training, etc. unplanned problems arise—a product launch fails, your largest vendor is acquired by your biggest competitor, someone gets sick, or in the military a weapon malfunctions. Let's say your company is out of compliance with its bank covenants. You feel pain—different from the physical pain one feels at BUD/S, or LUF, to be sure, but no less mental anguish. Overcoming the bank covenant issue, or missing your quarterly numbers to Wall Street analysts, is a hurdle or waypoint. You and your team must overcome the bank issue by working together via negotiations with the bank and changes to your business operations. But satisfying the bank or making your numbers is not the finish line. You must make adjustments and push on.

The challenge I experienced with my shoulder is small compared to problems the SEALs and/or business executives face on a regular basis. However, I believe the lesson is applicable to all—you adjust, make changes to overcome, and achieve your objective/mission.

I have participated in marathons, triathlons, and adventure races, and I always mentally played games with the distance involved, because I knew where the finish line was. In LUF, much like in life, combat, and business, one does not have a finish line, but more of a waypoint or benchmark. Upon reaching that point, you pivot, make adjustments, and continue. I did not understand the LUF mantra "there is no finish line" at first. We had no sense or control over the duration of each evolution. The lesson is invaluable, because each one of us has to continue to push and make progress in life and business. There is no game clock or goal line. The merger or product launch is a waypoint, not a finish line. Your job is never done!

One individual is capable of accomplishing a tremendous amount. But when you work with a team, and are able to lead and be *led,* there are no limitations. Anything is possible. Working with management teams that are aligned and motivated, much like our boat crews during LUF, one can build incredible enterprises.

Everyone has strengths and weaknesses, and the LUF experience highlights them. For example, the Smurfs or small guys (I am one) are quicker than the Big Reds (big guys) running on the sand or other similar sand evolutions. But the Big Reds are better during Log PT, running with their IBS boat and other strength evolutions. When you are on a team you help each other. With my injured shoulder, I depended on help from my boat crew on a few evolutions. Conversely, my team depended on me when someone else was struggling through an evolution. We worked together to accomplish our goals. In business, management needs to balance the utilization of assets, depending on speed, quality, and cost. Much like SEAL teams, management must recognize the differences—the strengths and weaknesses—in the Smurf Crew and the Big Red boat crew. Both are vital, but serve different purposes. The key is to know when to use what boat crew, management team, and/or employee. You must decide what asset or product best achieves your goal or mission.

*M***iguel Garat** *is founder and CEO of HWS Group, a full-service contract dealer focused on the corporate, hospitality, education, and health-care segments.*

I have lived and worked in China for the past ten years. China, as most business leaders know, is what I would call a "chronically" uncertain market where agility is an exceptionally powerful and competitive weapon. Right now it's a fantastic time to be in business but this market, due to its uncertainty, is very tactical and requires talented people in the field who can quickly sense and analyze market changes and then jump quickly into implementation.

I have seen many of my competitors make a decision and then not execute it because they kept debating it after it was made. In my company, when a manager makes a decision it sticks. We don't allow second-guessing.

At Haworth when I was the managing director for Greater China and North Asia, and now in my own company, I always asked myself: how can I grow the business as fast as we need to without destroying our company? This is primarily related to finding the right people in an uncertain market like China where talent is expensive and very difficult to find.

Here are some of the things we do:

- When we recruit, we focus on cultural fit.

- We hire people who are sharp, motivated, and respond positively to change.

- Managers are required to make decisions quickly.

- Those decisions stick and second-guessing is not allowed.

- We celebrate collaboration, which involves free flow of information and quick decision-making in a flat organization structure.

PASSION CAN MOVE
MOUNTAINS

ONE THING ABOUT being a Navy SEAL: I never had to wonder if I was making a real difference in this world. My life had a clear purpose. I was keeping America safe, doling out justice to those who needed to be taken down, and having a helluva good time fighting and training with some of the fiercest warriors on the planet.

My leaders and teammates felt the same way. And because of that, I was filled with professional and personal passion. It was easy to get fired up each and every day. My postmilitary career is also something I'm incredibly passionate about. Those fires are still burning.

Passion has always helped me lead others with more clarity, commitment, and moral courage. Passion fuels my spirit and focuses my vision. It's also infectious. Clients tell me constantly that my palpable passion for helping them to become better leaders motivates and inspires them. They say the same sorts of things about my cadre.

These accomplished business executives know I'm not doing shtick or performance when I'm rallying them to a cause or animatedly leading them to some finish line. It's not about yelling and screaming or theatrics or histrionics. It's not even about motivation or cheerleading. It's inspiring, don't get me wrong, but true passion is much deeper than that. Those I work with know how deeply I care about the notion of leadership and the power of dynamic teams. They also know how much I want them to benefit from that passion. They see that my day-to-day actions consistently bear that out. My deep belief in them and in my mission is as clear as the San Diego sky. As a result, they are loyal and eager and willing to follow and, more important, to grow.

I learned in the SEALs that people are more apt to deeply commit to a vision or a mission—and even a leader—if they sense that leader's genuine passion for a cause. That's especially true in perilous times, whether in the boardroom or on the battlefield. Passion makes others feel like they are working not *for* someone but, rather, *with* others— and working *for something bigger* than the individuals involved.

If you have passion you can ignite passion in others. That said, when you can focus your passion—something I've admittedly been challenged with over my own entrepreneurial endeavors—you're much better equipped to create vision.

So, how do you go about firing up your passion?

For starters, you've got to believe in . . . something. You've got to find the meaning and significance in who you are or what you do. Most SEALs I know wanted to challenge themselves—physically, emotionally, intellectually—and to make a difference. Their enthusiasm— their passion—sprang from there. What are you passionate about? Or what *were* you *once* passionate about and want to get back in touch with? Figure that out and start running with it. It's high time to be all you used to be.

Next, you need to have the right people around you. SEAL teams rarely lack passionate leadership. And it comes from the top down. Our leaders live and exude passion, and it permeates the entire organization. In the corporate world, I've learned, it's especially important for companies to hire the right kinds of people—people with commitment. As the old saying goes, it's far better to have one person with passion than forty who are merely interested. Before you let someone on the bus, find out what inspires them. What do they love about what they do? What do they believe in? While experience and education count for a lot, passion should be at the top of your hiring criteria. Consider it a tangible asset.

In the SEALs, BUD/S is where our "hiring managers" are able to vet the passionate from the poseurs, the whiners from the winners, and the motivated from the malcontent. On graduation day, we know we're pushing passionate people out into the fleet. In our world, no one robotically just shows up for work, punches a time card, or just kills time waiting for quitting time. Instead, we can't wait to try out new weapons, jump out of perfectly good airplanes, or rehearse close-quarters combat drills. We're downright giddy about getting going each morning. We feel deeply committed to our mission, our teammates, and our country. Having such top-down and bottom-up buy-in is critical.

Last, you've got to do more leading and less managing. Be a visible and motivating presence. Know your people and what drives them. Know what they need to be more successful both at work and off the clock and do what you can to support both. Be a great communicator. Create and drive a vision that others will lock on to and follow. Embrace creative, innovative, and inclusive cultures—flex time, anyone?—that enable others to flourish and succeed. In short, spread your passion around.

I'm a big believer in supporting passions other than work. I'm always looking for new ways to recharge my personal batteries. One amazing way came in the summer of 2013, when I was afforded a life-changing opportunity that ignited an entirely new passion for me: environmentalism. I eagerly talked about it in an interview that I gave to the *San Diego Union Tribune* at the time.

I was contacted by Craig Sawyer, a former SEAL colleague of mine, and a group of producers from the Animal Planet network. They wanted to develop a cable TV miniseries where four Special Forces experts would take on the brutal poachers who are bringing rhinos to the brink of extinction in South Africa.

The result: *Battleground: Rhino Wars,* which documented the intense conflict in protecting rhinos as a result of worldwide commercial demand for rhino horns—an exotic commodity that's more valuable than gold on South Africa's black market.

Craig and the folks from Animal Planet asked me to join a team of two other former Navy SEALs, and deploy to just north of Johannesburg. The three-part miniseries revealed the fierce and bloody conflict between the poachers and the South African antipoaching unit we would support. Our mission: do what we could to help stop the illegal but incredibly lucrative trade of rhino horns. It was the sort of bloody war where both rhinos and people are being slaughtered with increasingly regularity. Each year, more than five hundred rhinos are killed, experts say, and the situation is getting worse.

For two months, Craig and I were joined by former SEAL sniper Jeff Biggs and an active-duty medic known only as "Oz." Our battleground: the sprawling Kruger National Park. We worked alongside an antipoaching security company to try to catch and deter the men who slaughter these magnificent rhinos for their coveted horns. We helped train the antipoaching forces, conducted critical surveys, and exchanged tactical information in an effort to defeat the poachers.

While gathering intelligence on and tracking and stalking our human prey were not unlike typical SEAL work, the fact we that we had to look for these armed and dangerous dudes while also avoiding lions and other African beasts was an entirely new and amazing experience.

My job on the team was to serve as the intel expert. While Craig and the other boys hunkered down every day in the bush hunting or waiting to ambush poachers, it was my job to find out about these kinds of attacks before they occurred. I was out pressing the flesh, assuming multiple identities and running in some very dark urban areas. I infiltrated the dangerous underworld of the poachers, scouring the local marketplaces and black-market hideouts in search of actionable intelligence my team could use to thwart future rhino attacks. I'd bribe some bad guys, bully some others, all while ferreting out as much raw intel as I could. Then I'd spend hours poring over the data trying to make sense of it all. When I hit pay dirt, I'd call it in to my teammates for action. It was dangerous work. Anytime you mess with a criminal syndicate things are dicey. People were being killed all around us. We were told that more than one hundred park rangers and security forces had been killed by poachers over the years.

I found myself becoming incredibly passionate about this new and important mission I was immersed in. It was fueled by both the crew of Animal Planet, as well as the antipoaching forces we were supporting. When I watched a segment of film showing a baby rhino baying—crying, really—over its mother's dead and hornless corpse, that passion became a calling. All of the hardships and frustrations my team faced in the course of our deployment were nothing compared to the anger I felt at these brutal poachers.

As in the SEALs, I saw that my presence and talents had a real impact. While we didn't stop the poaching completely—and to be honest, our show was as much about awareness as actual antipoaching—we stemmed the tide a bit. And I can tell my kids and my grandkids that I helped to raise awareness of the plight of the rhino, and that my efforts may have helped save some of them now and in the future. We arrested a few bad guys and we exploited their networks a bit, and I played a real part in that. And who knows, like I told the newspaper reporters, maybe it will become my calling to be a full-time environmentalist someday.

Remember the words of French Field Marshal Ferdinand Foch: "The most powerful weapon on earth is the human soul on fire."

Go on. Light yourself on fire. You'll be amazed at the number of people who line up to watch you burn.

THE SIX PRINCIPLES
OF SUCCESSFUL
SPECIAL OPERATIONS

RECENTLY RETIRED, Vice Admiral William H. McRaven is the ninth commander of United States Special Operations Command (USSOCOM), headquartered at MacDill Air Force Base, in Florida. He is also a legendary Navy SEAL. McRaven and his troopers worked to "ensure the readiness of joint special operations forces and, as directed, conduct operations worldwide."

McRaven, if you recall, stepped out of the shadows in 2011 following the successful raid on Osama bin Laden's Pakistani compound. Based on intelligence gathered by the CIA, McRaven—then the commander of Joint Special Operations Command (JSOC), headquartered at Fort Bragg, North Carolina—led the JSOC team that planned and executed the commando raid, dubbed Operation Neptune Spear.

At the direction of the president, McRaven and his team spent nearly four months developing myriad options for the raid, convincing a jittery president and members of the National Security Council and other senior government leaders that the mission could be successful, and conducting detailed mission rehearsals. It was an exercise in cool, calculated, and confident combat leadership that McRaven had spent a lifetime and storied career preparing for.

McRaven, to no one's surprise, chose my trusted old unit—Naval Special Warfare Development Group (DEVGRU), also known as SEAL Team Six, to lead Neptune Spear.

On May 2, 2011, after finally getting the go-ahead from the White House, DEVGRU SEALs dispatched bin Laden "for God and country," as the SEAL team raid leader radioed McRaven upon confirmation of the terrorist mastermind's death.

McRaven's leadership under fire was no surprise in professional military circles. In his thirty-seven-year career, he's led, planned, or participated in scores of even more complicated, complex, and harrowing missions. In that time, McRaven has commanded at every level within the Special Operations community, including assignments as deputy commanding general for operations at JSOC; commodore of Naval Special Warfare Group One; commander of SEAL Team Three; task group commander in the US Central Command area of responsibility; task unit commander during Desert Storm and Desert Shield; squadron commander at DEVGRU; and SEAL platoon commander at Underwater Demolition Team 21/SEAL Team Four.

He served as the director for strategic planning in the Office of Combating Terrorism on the National Security Council staff; assessment director at USSOCOM, on the staff of the chief of naval operations, and as the chief of staff at Naval Special Warfare Group One. After having left the Navy in 2014, McRaven is reportedly going to become chancellor of the University of Texas system.

In 1995, McRaven published a popular book on covert missions called *Spec Ops: Case Studies in Special Operations Warfare: Theory and Practice*. It's a thrilling compendium of eight raids, rescues, and assaults—including the 1976 Israeli rescue of hostages from Uganda's Entebbe airport—by SEALs and other special operators such as the Green Berets, Britain's Special Air Service, and Russia's Spetsnaz.

As he described in the book—and as I've been teaching business leaders for years—preparation, firepower, speed on target, and moral commitment give highly motivated teams the ultimate edge over their opponents.

McRaven shows how a small team of soldiers can attack a numerically superior force in an entrenched position and succeed, thanks to what he believes are the six essential principles of Special Operations: simplicity, security, repetition, surprise, speed, and purpose.

Here are a few excerpts from McRaven's book that can help enlighten any leader. I highly recommend reading *Spec Ops,* as well as German soldier and military theorist Carl von Clausewitz.

USE THE KISS METHOD—KEEP IT SIMPLE, STUPID: "Simplicity is the most crucial, and yet sometimes the most difficult, principle with which to comply. How does one make a plan simple? There are three elements of simplicity critical to success: limiting the number of objectives, good intelligence, and innovation.

". . . It is essential to limit the number of tactical objectives to only those that are vital. Limiting the objectives to only what is essential focuses the training, limits the number of personnel required, reduces the time on target, and decreases the number of 'moving parts.'"

PUT YOUR PLANS TO THE TEST: "It is essential to conduct at least one, and preferably two, full-dress rehearsals prior to the mission. The plan that sounded simple on paper must now be put to the test. The need for a full-dress rehearsal is borne out time and again. Invariably when a certain aspect of an operation was not rehearsed, it failed during the actual mission."

McRaven's advice reminds me of a quote from bestselling author Malcom Gladwell on the matter of practice. "Basketball is an intricate, high-speed game filled with split-second, spontaneous decisions. But that spontaneity is possible only when everyone first engages in hours of highly repetitive and structured practice—perfecting their shooting, dribbling, and passing and running plays over and over again—and agrees to play a carefully defined role on the court. . . . [S]pontaneity isn't random."

SURPRISE: "Many tacticians consider the principle of surprise to be the most important factor in a successful special operation. They mistakenly believe that it is surprise that gives them the decisive advantage over the enemy, as if merely catching the enemy unprepared would assure the attacking force of victory. This is not the case. Surprise is useless and indeed unachievable without the other principles. What good would it do to surprise the enemy, only to be ill equipped to fight him? Surprise is essential, but it should not be viewed in isolation."

THE NEED FOR SPEED: "Speed in a special operation is a function of time, not, as some imply, a relative factor that is affected by the enemy's will to resist. Relative superiority can be gained, despite the efforts of the enemy, primarily because the attacking force moves with such speed that the enemy's reaction is not an overriding factor."

BE IN IT TO WIN IT: "Purpose is understanding and then executing the prime objective of the mission regardless of the emerging obstacles or opportunities. There are two aspects to this principle. First, the purpose must be clearly defined by the mission statement: rescue the POWs, destroy the dry dock, sink the battleship, etc. This mission statement should be crafted to ensure that in the heat of battle, no matter what else happens, the individual soldier understands the primary objective.

"The second aspect of the principle is personal commitment. The purpose of the mission must be thoroughly understood beforehand, and the men must be inspired with a sense of personal dedication that knows no limitations.

"In an age of high technology and Jedi Knights we often overlook the need for personal involvement, but we do so at our own risk. As Clausewitz warned, 'Theorists are apt to look on fighting in the abstract as a trial of strength without emotion entering into it. This is one of a thousand errors which they quite consciously commit because they have no idea of the implications.'"

In the conclusion of *Spec Ops,* McRaven circles back to perhaps the most essential element of the Special Operations raids that he writes about: the people on the teams.

"They understood the importance of detailed planning, constant rehearsals, and precise execution. . . . The officers and enlisted whom I interviewed were professionals who fully appreciated the value of proper planning and preparations, of good order and discipline, and of working with higher authorities. They were also exceptionally modest men who felt that there was nothing heroic in their actions and often sought to downplay their public image."

Hooyah.

YOU NEED A VISION

T HE BEST AND MOST SUCCESSFUL leaders I have ever met have the "vision" thing: Big ideas. Daring dreams. Gargantuan gambles.

Like a properly oriented military map identifying hills, ridges, valleys, saddles, and depressions, a vision captures exactly where a leader and the business want to go. Unlike a plan, which spells out in painstaking detail exactly how to get "there," a vision provides the inspiring direction and heading for the daily operations of your business. And because it helps you know what "right" looks like, a stated vision also helps shape strategic decision-making.

In essence, a corporate vision is the articulated ideal that sets the tone for a successful business endeavor. The best ones are both aspirational and inspirational—just like the image of a Navy SEAL or the cover model of a fitness magazine. Visions are also easy to understand, but that certainly doesn't mean they are unsophisticated. A leader who can express the essence of their company in a simple, unambiguous way is highly sophisticated in my book.

When I was a SEAL, my vision of who we were and what we did was the reason I got out of bed each morning and slept well each night. It's the same for me now in my entrepreneurial endeavors. Visions are the rallying cry—and rally point—for highly motivated, truly dedicated employees and loyal customers. They are broad and insightful. They are anything but tactical. They define our place in the world.

A vision also defines what the world would lose if you and your business did not exist.

So, do you have a vision? If so, have you shared it with the world or, at the very least, the people who work for you? If you answered "no" to either of these questions, then drop and give me twenty. Too slow! Drop and do it again! After you have paid the man (that's me, by the way), and before you do anything else—even before you turn the next page of this book—I want you to sit down and pound out the vision you have for your company or for the division/department you are responsible for. It need not be long. A sentence or a paragraph is more than sufficient.

Until you do this, the dynamic teams that you and I are trying so hard to create will continue to underperform. They will be unable to move forward in any dynamic way and will instead be stuck putting out small fires. They won't dream big and develop or execute bold strategies and plans in support of the vision. Conversely, if the vision is clear and sound, decisions can be made more quickly and more easily because they are informed by your vision. They actually make doing day-to-day business easier.

At SOT-G, my vision is very simple—to "continually provide value and to serve." That's it. Short, sweet, and to the point. There's nothing about process; instead, it's all about the payoff. I want to be a servant leader to others. My vision of providing value and service by help-ing organizations create teams that dazzle and excel is what drives me and my staff. That vision fuels us to do more than just put out small fires every day. Under that visionary umbrella, we're able to de-velop the company's mission and immerse ourselves in it. We help solve systemic leadership problems through innovative and realistic training. I custom design leadership training experiences for everyone from Honda Motor Company to the UCLA football team. That training is SOT-G's mission.

Again, a vision statement does not have to be long to be powerful. For example, Hilton Worldwide has, like SOT-G, a one-sentence vision: "To fill the earth with the light and warmth of hospitality." There's nothing mystical or pie-in-the-sky about that vision. It's poetic, to be sure, but it's firmly grounded in practical and realistic terms. It's strategically sound and a clear guiding principle. It's the grand idea—the ideal—from which Hilton's strategic priorities emanate. At the same time, the company's mission statement naturally flows from their vision: "To be the preeminent global hospitality company—the first choice of guests, team members, and owners alike."

Interestingly, America's military services routinely struggle with their visions for the future. The Army, Navy, Air Force, and Marines continually need to define their relevance in terms of roles and missions. It's a tough turf war at the highest levels, especially in times of fiscal austerity. For the SEALs, however, the vision rarely changes. The missions and strategies in support of the vision are continually changing, but the core vision of the organization is unchanging: We're the dirty guys who do the country's dirty jobs. We know who we are and where we're headed.

In order to lead, you have to know where you're going. As Lewis Carroll, author of *Alice's Adventures in Wonderland,* playfully said, "If you don't know where you are going, any road can take you there." As a leader, you want to drive the train. Having a vision is one of your core responsibilities. It's on you. Remember, I'm the guy who is here to tell you how to build successful teams. I'm not here to create your vision. That's beyond my scope and capacity. I can, however, loudly and confidently tell you how vitally important a vision is.

To that end, set the bar high. Remember what it is that drove you in the beginning when you first created your company, or when you were so motivated by a particular company that you decided to join it. Put that passion, that vision, down on paper right now. And, most important, be sure to share your vision with your employees. They need to know how they fit in, and how what they do contributes to the realization of your vision. Help them help you.

THE ESSENTIAL SEVEN

I RECENTLY READ A story in *Inc.* magazine that listed what it considered the seven characteristics of truly extraordinary teams. The list was gleaned from a conversation *Inc.* editors had with Phil Geldart, author of the book *In Your Hands: The Behaviors of a World-Class Leader.* I'm convinced that Geldart was a SEAL in a past life, because his list reinforces everything I've learned over two decades on the Teams. Here's the list, in all its uncomplicated and uncluttered glory.

1. Extraordinary teams have a clear leader.

2. Extraordinary teams have quantifiable goals.

3. Extraordinary teams have well-defined roles.

4. Extraordinary teams share resources.

5. Extraordinary teams communicate effectively.

6. Extraordinary teams are 100 percent committed.

7. Extraordinary teams discourage big egos.

THE LANGUAGE
OF LEADERSHIP

W HILE COMMUNICATION with your employees is a leadership imperative, it does little good if the language you use gets lost in translation.

When I talk to kids of the millennial generation, for example, I sometimes feel like I am talking to complete and utter strangers. For starters, they may be incredibly bright and adaptable, but they're also flaky. They are job-hoppers who distrust and dislike traditional hierarchical structures. I'm not saying they are right or wrong in their approach to life—it's just that they are very different than my baby boom and Gen X compadres. Because they are constantly "connected" to the Internet of Things, and increasingly dependent on social media, millennials are often isolationists, as odd as I know that sounds. What I mean is that when there's a problem with one thing or a question about another, they'd rather text me or email me than walk over and simply have a conversation. It's not that they don't like Rob; I get that. It's just that they prefer to communicate via technology rather than face-to-face.

When that difference in personal style is coupled with a language barrier, you can see the potential minefield that requires careful navigation. And the onus is on me—the leader—to be the one who communicates clearly and effectively. It's my job to span that cultural or generational divide.

The most important thing to remember is to always know your audience. People from different generations are motivated by different things and possess different values, attitudes, ideas, and methods for achieving success. Anecdotes, analogies, and cultural mentions are only powerful if the right context and reference is present. Baby boomers—those born in the years between 1947 and the early 1960s—speak and act differently than those from Generation X (1960s to 1980s), the Millennial Generation (1980s to 2000s), or what I've recently learned is the Z Generation (2000s to the present).

Not too long ago I was teaching advanced Visit, Board, Search, and Seizure tactics to young Navy sailors. These are the maritime boarding teams who conduct inspections designed to thwart piracy, smuggling, and terrorism or, in the worst case, actually seize vessels. It's dangerous, physical work that can quickly and unexpectedly turn from a routine, nonlethal inspection one minute to something akin to a knife fight in a phone booth in the next.

I warned the students that my staff would not hesitate to get physical with them in order to enhance the realism of the training. As I said this, I tried singing a few mangled bars from singer Olivia Newton-John's 1981 hit "Physical" to break the tension.

"We're gonna get physical . . . physical," I crooned. *"We're gonna get physicalllllllll. You're gonna hear our bodies talk . . . our bodies talk. . . ."*

Their reaction? Bewilderment. Complete and total bewilderment. I might have been a *Saturday Night Live* skit. I made no connection, had no impact, and ended up looking like a flake. Those under the age of forty-five had no knowledge of—or frame of reference for—that song, despite the fact that "Physical" went on to become the biggest-selling single of the decade in the United States! Like Olivia Newton-John herself, the reference has faded into complete obscurity. If I had been speaking to an AARP convention, I might have been a monster hit. To eighteen- and nineteen-year-old sailors, however, I was the odd man out.

Context is another matter. For example, there's a joke in the military that goes something like this: If you give the command "Secure the building," here is what the different services would do:

The NAVY will turn out the lights and lock the doors.

The ARMY will surround the building with defensive fortifications, tanks, and concertina wire.

The MARINE CORPS will assault the building, using overlapping fields of fire from all appropriate points on the perimeter.

The AIR FORCE will take out a three-year lease with an option to buy the building.

Culture—in this case service culture—is a real consideration when communicating. Words mean different things to different people.

More seriously, in his book *Fires & Furies: The L.A. Riots,* author James D. Delk showed how cultural language was nearly deadly in the 1992 Los Angeles riots, when military units were called up to support the city's police officers:

> *Police officers responded to a domestic dispute, accompanied by Marines. They had just gone up to the door when two shotgun birdshot rounds were fired through the door, hitting the officers. One yelled "cover me!" to the Marines, who then laid down a heavy base of fire. . . . The police officer had not meant "shoot" when he yelled "cover me" to the Marines. [He] meant . . . point your weapons and be prepared to respond if necessary. However, the Marines responded instantly in the precise way they had been trained, where "cover me" means provide me with cover using firepower. . . . over two hundred bullets [were] fired into that house.* [Thankfully, no one inside the house was injured in the incident.]

The mission of a Marine infantry squad is to locate, close with, and destroy the enemy by fire and maneuver, or to repel the enemy's assault by fire and close combat. A peace officer—a police officer—protects and serves. It's easy to see how words can be misconstrued in different cultures.

The bottom line: whether you're motivating or mentoring your teams, you must take time to clearly understand who it is you are talking to. Demographics matter. Better yet, the next time you communicate with your employees, don't forget the other important facet you're responsible for: be a great listener. Every one of your employees is unique and has value. Give them a voice and learn from their musings.

GET EVERYBODY ON
THE SAME PAGE

ANAVY SEAL TEAM is almost always more innovative and productive than any individual SEAL. But in order for the team to work effectively, every member must be on the same page. That's rarely a problem for us. We share a common vision and that results in clarity and commitment.

Once a mission has been briefed to the SEAL team, you can be damn sure that every member understands the team's mission and his role in it. More important, he understands every other SEAL's role and responsibility. That's what makes us so nimble and adaptable to any existing and emerging situations and, consequently, so devastatingly successful.

If a flag or general officer walked into our ready room and asked me about the mission at hand, I could confidently tell him or her everything they needed to know about the situation, mission, execution, administration, logistics, and command and signal. I know who has the C-4 and will blow down the doors, who will take point on infiltration, which man will be responsible for the interrogation of prisoners, and on and on down to who's buying the beers at the postgame party. The SEAL next to me could say the same thing. We'd also clarify our personal objectives as well as the objectives of the next SEAL in the operation. We all know what to do and who is doing what. We're on the same page. And that makes us crazy capable. And continually adaptable.

Consider an oarsman on an Athenian trireme during the Persian Wars. To defeat King Xerxes's invasion fleet, the Greeks relied on the orchestrated teamwork and effort of each of the 170 skilled, professional rowers who propelled their warships. The Athenian fleet's ability to reign supreme on the seas was in large part due to the coordinated abilities, knowledge, and execution of their trireme teams. The crews were all on the same page, in the same moment.

Your own organization needs to operate in the very same manner. If the CEO of Our Cars Inc.—a company comprising fourteen automotive dealerships—has a vision of "The Customer Is Always First," for example, then every Sea Stallion employee must know that and embody it in everything they do. If the employee who mans a dealership parking lot or washes the cars there does not understand that sensibility, then the corporate mission fails. It fails because those employees who are often the very first point of contact for the majority of the general public are not on the same page as everyone else. Consequently, they are unequipped to preach the corporate gospel, let alone uphold the standard. Even worse: by not communicating, a void may be created that, as a British naval historian once said, could soon be "filled with poison, drivel and misrepresentation."

The critical requirement to getting everyone on the same page is for leadership to share ideas and information. A leader can't expect to inspire action or create urgency in others if they don't. By openly sharing information, trusting their teammates, and by establishing clear standards and expectations, a leader creates the common cause. She's using the very language of leadership. She's communicating.

COMMIT TO
COMMITMENT

THERE'S NOTHING that frustrates me more than someone who fails to give 100 percent effort, 100 percent of the time.

If you're going to show up, show up. If you're not going to show up, don't show up.

THE ELEMENTS OF THE WARRIOR MINDSET

To HAVE THE MINDSET of a warrior, one must:

1. Be inclusive, not exclusive.

2. Share information with those who have less than you do.

3. Possess uncompromising integrity.

4. Have both moral and physical courage.

5. Be prepared to act, and not simply react.

6. Be willing to lead.

7. Train your replacements.

AN EXPECTATION
OF SUCCESS

IF I HAD TO USE one business word or term to describe the SEAL brand, my choice would be *excellence.*

SEALs have an expectation of excellence—not only for their teams but for themselves, too. It's a hard-won habit that has transformed into a worldwide expectation. We are what we repeatedly do, as the philosopher Aristotle said. SEAL excellence, then, is not an act, but a habit. I don't care if it's writing a report, doing PT, or conducting a raid; day-to-day excellence—in every task—is an expectation.

In order to achieve excellence, to be truly superior, SEALs realize there can be no excuses. We know that we just need to get . . . this . . . shit . . . done. Period. Whatever that is! You can count on us. We're reliable.

It helps that we're motivated by our cause, but intestinal fortitude is also an integral factor. It's our armor against boredom, our fort against distraction. Fortitude lets us see it through. For we know that true success lies not in the talking, but in the doing, whatever the circumstances. Cold, wet, tired, hard, or hurt, it doesn't matter. We push through it all and get the mission accomplished. We will die—or die trying—before we quit. Simply put: we persevere. That's because we know there is no elevator to success. You have to take the stairs.

Turn off those inner voices that say something's too hard, too complicated, too time-consuming, or even not worth doing. It's time you stop being afraid of the risks or the possible consequences and complications. Do what others cannot or will not do. Commit yourself to personal and professional excellence and a "get it done" mentality. It's a powerful double tap.

ADAPTABILITY

A S I VISIT VARIOUS COMPANIES, I frequently see a poster that says "Innovate or Die." I like the mantra a lot and believe in the sensibility. But from a SEALs standpoint, "Adapt or Die" makes more sense.

The importance of adaptability is built in to the acronym of our organization. *SE*a, *A*ir, *L*and: SEALs train and work just about anywhere you can imagine in the air, on land, or at sea, including desert and urban areas, mountains and woodlands, and jungle and arctic conditions. We pride ourselves on anticipating shifts in the world and changes in technology and fiercely fight for new and innovative ways to deal with it. We think creatively and boldly. We have the vision and the insight to see that the world and technology are constantly changing and we remain ever flexible, ever adaptable. I do the same as a leadership coach, and my training seminars reflect it.

In BUD/S, SEAL students learn to adapt to their surroundings each and every day. When I was there, we had to adapt in order just to survive our instructors. We had to figure out how to get to the chow hall faster each day, for example, or we'd suffer the consequences. We had to learn when to give some event our all, and when to throttle back. Or not. No one told us how to do these things. We had to figure it out—to adapt. After showing up at the wrong event one too many times, we quickly learned to pay strict attention to detail on things like daily training schedules, where changes were continually being made. It was on us to expect and anticipate changes and to adapt accordingly. We never groused about it. It was what it was. If things got painful, we adjusted and adapted our bodies to the pain and kept on going. What's the mission, instructor?

For SEALs, our adaptive abilities can often mean the difference between life and death. When you are fighting on death ground, firepower helps a lot, but it's rapid, creative thinking that will save you. Therefore, SEALs believe in the ancient Chinese proverb "The wise man adapts himself to circumstances as water shapes itself to the vessel that contains it."

In 2000, the Army Research Institute for Behavioral Sciences described many of the behaviors that leaders in Special Operations units like the Navy SEALs exhibit. Researchers defined adaptability as *making an effective change in response to a change in the situation.* That's a pretty apt description, in my book. While individuals differed in their ability to adapt, researchers found, adaptability is a skill that can be taught and trained. I've made a living in the corporate world proving that.

Here's how the Army researchers described the various elements of adaptive behavior and some things you can use to become more adaptable in your own life.

- HANDLING EMERGENCIES OR CRISIS SITUATIONS—
  Reacting with appropriate urgency in life-threatening, dangerous, or emergency situations; quickly analyzing options and making split-second decisions based on clear and focused thinking; maintaining emotional control and objectivity while keeping focused on the situation at hand.

- HANDLING WORK STRESS—Remaining composed and cool when faced with difficult circumstances or a highly demanding workload; managing frustration well by directing efforts to constructive solutions; demonstrating resilience and the highest levels of professionalism in stressful circumstances; acting as a calming and settling influence to whom others look for guidance.

- SOLVING PROBLEMS CREATIVELY—Turning problems upside down and inside out to generate new, innovative ideas; thinking outside the given parameters and integrating seemingly unrelated information to develop creative solutions; developing innovative methods of obtaining or using resources when there are insufficient resources.

- DEALING WITH UNCERTAIN AND UNPREDICTABLE WORK SITUATIONS—Effectively adjusting plans, goals, actions, or priorities to deal with changing situations; imposing structure for self and others that provides as much focus as possible in changing situations; refusing to be paralyzed by uncertainty or ambiguity.

- LEARNING WORK TASKS, TECHNOLOGIES, AND PROCEDURES—Demonstrating enthusiasm for and proficiently learning new approaches and technologies for conducting work; anticipating changes in the work demands and searching for and participating in assignments or training that will prepare self for these changes.

- DEMONSTRATING INTERPERSONAL ADAPTABILITY— Considering others' viewpoints and opinions and altering own opinion when it is appropriate to do so; being open and accepting of negative or developmental feedback regarding work; demonstrating keen insight of others' behavior and tailoring own behavior to persuade, influence, or work more effectively with them.

- DEMONSTRATING CULTURAL ADAPTABILITY—Taking action to learn about and understand the climate, orientation, needs, and values of other groups, organizations, or cultures; understanding the implications of one's actions and adjusting approach to maintain positive relationships with other groups, organizations, or cultures.

- DEMONSTRATING PHYSICALLY ORIENTED ADAPTABILITY—Adjusting to challenging environmental states such as extreme heat, humidity, or cold; adjusting weight and muscular strength or becoming proficient in performing physical tasks for the job.

Becoming more adaptable also includes knowing yourself and your own strengths and weaknesses. Self-awareness, as I have said before, is a gift from God. If you understand the beliefs and values that drive your behaviors, you'll be better able to adapt to change and respond when a change in thinking is required.

I've always benefited from being flexible in my approach to things. *Semper Gumby,* as my Marine friends like to say. "Always flexible." By having a flexible mindset, it means I don't always expect things to go a certain way—or my way all the time. I'm open and ready for any possibility. I also deal in options, not ultimatums. I have a backup plan to the backup plan. Lastly, having a positive attitude is a key factor in being adaptable. I'm also not afraid of change—in the boardroom or on the battlefield. Change has always helped me grow as a person. The adaptable leader sees change as necessary and good.

EXECUTING A PLAN

1. Get *very* clear on the objective.

   – Ask clarifying questions.

2. Identify all the resources you have at your disposal that can help you execute the plan.

3. Clarify roles and responsibilities.

4. Everything you do should be designed to forward the goals of the mission.

5. Anticipate what could go wrong and develop a contingency plan.

   – Be deliberate as you evaluate your plan; critically look at/ adjust your plan.

   – How are you monitoring your plan to judge if it's working?

6. Execute with speed.

   – Don't rush, as it will create mistakes, but do not waste time moving toward your objective.

7. Debrief with the team after executing and completing the plan.

   – What did you learn?

   – What went well?

   – What could have been done better?

HUMAN RESOURCES— A SEALS PERSPECTIVE

- People are the most important resource on SEAL teams.

  - Each SEAL is worth $25 million (the amount of money invested in their training).

- Win as a team. Lose as a team.

  - Your team is only as fast as your slowest man.

  - It's not about the individual.

- Support each other. Take care of your people.

- Assign mentors (more on this shortly).

  - All new SEALs are assigned a veteran mentor.

  - All SEALs have a responsibility to serve as a mentor at some point in time.

  - Commanding officers ensure that mentors do their jobs and help new SEALs.

- Identify and advance talent.

- SEALs have no time for people trying to protect their own job by holding subordinates back.

- A team must stick together when things go bad. Once a team fractures, things go south really fast.

MENTAL TOUGHNESS

- Find the calm amid the chaos.

- Be decisive. Move quickly.

- Don't let stress result in you blaming others.

- Don't let distractions deter you from accomplishing your objectives.

- Never "take yourself out of the game." Always stay positive.

- Under stress, good leaders learn how to compartmentalize tasks so they don't get overwhelmed and shut down.

- Stay focused on the mission. Don't let fatigue or stress deter your focus.

TEAMWORK

- You must have great communication.

  - Span of Control: You can effectively communicate with six or seven people on a consistent basis.

  - What are your tools for communication?

  - It is critically important to let somebody know when they are letting the team down so that their actions can be corrected.

- How are decisions made?

  - Collect the needed data.

  - Make the decision as quickly as the situation requires.

- How does the team react when things are not going well?

PERFORMANCE EXPECTATIONS

- Give at least 100 percent, 100 percent of the time.

- If your leaders are failing the team, remove them quickly and replace them with someone who can get the job done.

- Get it right every single time . . . there is no tolerance for error.

- In the SEALs, if someone screws up in our line of work, people may die.

KNOW WHO YOU ARE

To succeed as a SEAL—to succeed as a leader in any organization—it is imperative that you know who you are. Consider the prophetic words of Sun Tzu: "If you know the enemy and know yourself, you need not fear the result of a hundred battles. If you know yourself but not the enemy, for every victory gained you will also suffer a defeat. If you know neither the enemy nor yourself, you will succumb in every battle."

The reality is that it takes hard, continuous work to really know oneself; to know one's strengths and weaknesses. But smart leaders funnel the same energy, passion, and competitiveness that they apply to the challenges in their everyday lives and they routinely turn it inward—focusing on knowing themselves better in order to gain a leadership advantage.

Consequently, these are the leaders who remember the life lessons that matter—and that also help others. They can easily recite their own dreams and aspirations. They understand their own temperament and are all too aware of the length of their personal fuse. They know what frustrates themselves *about* themselves as well as what frustrates them about other people. They know what motivates them to succeed—money, power, respect?—and what propels them to failure—ego, lust, greed? They deftly play to their strengths and fiercely fight to transcend their fears. They know their values and, consequently, know what it is that they will never compromise.

This isn't some exercise in navel-gazing. This is about knowing who you are so that you can better help yourself and be more prepared to help others.

When you are a SEAL, self-awareness heightens your ability to read situations more carefully and to then act and react accordingly. With self-awareness, your leadership is more evenhanded and steady. It won't sway in the wind, be affected by the crowd or the brushfires erupting all around you. If you know who you are and what you're made of, it's easier to serve those you lead with more vision, purpose, and clarity.

For example, if you know you have a tendency to be a fixer and not a delegator, you can take a deep breath, be contemplative, and consider multiple options when something goes wrong and requires your attention or direction. If you've ever taken the Myers-Briggs personality test, for example, you know that everyone has their own unique psychological type. None are better or worse, just different in many cases. Therefore, if you know that you are an ESTJ type (extroverted, sensing, thinking, judgment type), chances are you won't want to hire an INFP type (introverted, intuition, feeling, perception type) as your number two. Or maybe you would. It all depends on how that individual can shore up your own position as a leader. Who knows, after much thought and careful consideration, you may decide a touchy-feely sort is just the person you need to smooth out or make up for your own shortcomings in some particular area.

When you are not self-aware, you are prone to making poor decisions that can dramatically affect your life and career. If you overlook a vital aspect of who you are when making a career choice, for example, it could be disastrous for everyone involved.

When I was going through BUD/S (and as I routinely train clients in my stress-inducing classes and seminars), I quickly discovered that whether you left SEAL training as a graduate or a failure, you ultimately knew who you were. Those who didn't *really* want to be a SEAL soon figured that out. They didn't want to suffer the deprivations, the pain, or the mental anguish. Once they came to that realization about themselves—for some it takes a day; for others, it might take six weeks—they rang the Bell three times and placed their helmet on the deck. They dropped on request. They had a "come to Jesus" conversation with themselves and determined that being a SEAL really wasn't who they were or what they really wanted in life, painful as it might be to admit. And they moved on.

I know a journalist who is one of the best national security correspondents in the country. He's covered the lives and careers of soldiers, sailors, airmen, and marines for more than twenty-five years. He's been to the bottom of the ocean in deep-submersible vehicles, flown in fixed-wing fighter aircraft, stood on the outside deck of a nuclear-powered ballistic missile submarine as it prowled off the coast of Guam, smoked cigars while standing in the crow's nest of a heavy cruiser, and more. You name it, he's done it and he's loved every minute of it. It's a true passion and he's a great fit at the company he works for. Unfortunately, very few people outside the military have ever heard of the paper he works for (*Army Times*), and fewer still know my friend's name. That bothered him, he admitted over a beer one night. All journalists, I've learned, are somewhat self-impressed. They are some of the smartest, cleverest, and most creative people I know, but they all have healthy egos, some more than others.

Several years ago, frustrated, my friend thought about going to work for the *Washington Post* or *USA Today*. He started working his professional contacts, arranging interviews with key editors, and laying the groundwork for a possible career move. He was confident he had the skills required for such a move. He knew he could hang with the big boys. It wasn't a matter of whether he was qualified for the gig but rather, should the stars of opportunity align themselves, whether it would be a good personal and professional fit. Did he really want it? And then he had an honest conversation with himself. And the answer he came up with surprised him.

"I honestly realized that the real reason I wanted to work at the *Washington Post* was so that I could go to a dinner party and say to anyone who would listen: 'I'm a reporter for the *Washington Post*,'" my friend told me. "It was all about my ego."

As a husband and father of three young sons who enjoyed time with his family as much as any story he might be sent to cover, my friend knew what would happen if he jumped ship to the *Washington Post* or *USA Today*. It would mean more and longer hours in the office and in the field, for starters. And since he would be the junior employee on a staff of highly competitive veteran journalists, it would likely mean less juicy assignments—at least in the beginning. It would mean being on call twenty-four hours a day—365 days a year—given the requirements of a national, daily news organization. It would mean he would be all in, all the time.

"I knew what it would take to play at that level," he said. "And, in the end, I didn't want to give it. I realized that being where I was, was the very best thing for me at that particular time. I loved the company I worked for. I liked the people and the culture. I was well compensated. I had a great office and could pretty much come and go as I pleased.

"I didn't want a new job. My ego just wanted a stroke! I realized how childish I was being, but I'm glad I took the time to do the introspection and figure it out."

Had he not been honest with himself, it could have been a terrible decision. These sorts of awakenings happen all the time at BUD/S. Sometimes the instructors discover that the life and lifestyle of a SEAL are not right for someone. Most of the time, however, it's a personal discovery. In some cases, that little voice inside a SEAL candidate's head that's telling them they really don't want "it" that badly is telling them the truth. The stress and hardship of SEAL training always exposes a person's commitment.

I want you to take regular journeys of self-discovery. Reflect on some recent decisions you've made and the actions you have taken. Are they what you want or expect from yourself? If not, why not? Have the courage to ask others to give you honest feedback, even if it means you don't like what you find out. Ask others the same questions you ask of yourself: "Am I a good leader? Am I trustworthy? Am I inspiring?"

Only when we know ourselves can we ever hope to get the best from ourselves and those we are blessed to lead. Only then can we create SEAL-worthy teams.

LEAD FROM THE FRONT

I F YOU WANT OTHERS to follow you, you've got to lead by example. For SEALs, that means being able and willing to lead from the
front.

When you lead in this manner, you are showing your subordinates
that you will share their burdens; that you will fight shield to shield
on the front lines of combat. You are promising through your actions,
not just your words, that you will not be one of those faceless, sometimes heartless, souls positioned far from the action—in the rear
with the gear—issuing commands and ultimatums with no regard
for those who must do the real fighting. When you're at the front, you
know what's going on. You know what others are going through. You
get it.

In my time in the SEALs and in my time at SOT-G, never, under
any circumstances, would I ever ask any of my teammates to do anything that I was unable or unwilling to do myself. In fact, I've often
done my job as well as someone else's, just so others can gauge the
depth of that personal commitment. It's an ongoing, lifelong personal
campaign of learning for me, and I learned it from some of the best
leaders in the Navy. The way I figure it, how can I know what someone else is experiencing—and demand something extraordinary of
them—if I don't honestly know what it is that they do?

The visibility and physical commitment of a leader are critical to the culture and success of any organization, military or civilian. The leader must clearly be vested in the team and not be someone standing on the sidelines. He must be a full-share partner with an active role. Only then can he command the proper respect necessary for true, "follow-me" leadership. Only then can he truly understand and properly address the needs and the desires of those he most depends upon for mission success.

When you lead from the front you're showing others that their roles—their lives—are of equal value to yours. And they are, in the grand scheme of mission success. And when you are present, you also have a chance to set the bar high in terms of personal expectations of excellence. In this sort of culture, it's not the leader and *the others*. It's the leader as part of the team. The leader does not lord over anyone else. When you fight shoulder to shoulder with your troops in the trenches, you make it clear that all are needed in order to accomplish the mission.

But remember, this is not about some show of force or inspiration. It's not a stump speech at the annual employee picnic. It's much more regular and routine and certainly more genuine than that. You've got to take the time required to really get to know your people and what they do for the organization. Trust me, it's a wise investment, regardless of how painful and perfunctory such interaction may initially seem to you.

There are practical considerations and advantages to this culture as well. For example, when a leader is on the ground, in the mix, they have greater situational awareness of people, platforms, and potential problems. The perceptions and observations a leader makes are firsthand and not filtered or influenced by others. That quantifiably reduces the chances of miscommunication or misunderstanding. Conversely, when a leader lacks the interpersonal skills or the motivation to lead from the front, they miss essential opportunities for greater team success. It's hard to listen to the problems, concerns, or innovative solutions of motivated team members when the leader prefers to remain cloistered in their corner office.

It's hard for a leader to earn the respect of others when the leader is perceived to be shirking the heavy lifting. Nothing is more poisonous to a team than the thought that a leader is coasting while everyone else on the team is required to put out.

I remember a team leader we were once assigned when I was in BUD/S. This guy was the son of a very famous right-wing radio talk show host who was popular with the SEAL community at the time. Unfortunately, this apple had fallen very far from the tree. Every day he made it clear by his actions that he was there for himself and no one else. A classic "one-wayer" sort of guy. Personalities aside, this fellow didn't share the same burdens as the rest of our team. He never ran one evolution with our class. That's because he'd developed shin splints or something and by the third phase of training, he was riding a stationary bike full-time when the rest of us were out on the beach pounding sand. Worse yet, he once had the audacity to rat us out to the instructors after we had sprinted off for a required six-mile run without waiting for an instructor to give us the okay. Forget the fact that we actually ran the six miles. As punishment, the instructors called us together and railed on us for not following proper procedure. They then forced us out on another six-mile jaunt. Anyway, my point is simple. A leader must be—and must be seen as being—part of the team for true unit cohesion to grow and success to occur.

Studies have shown that a lack of leader interaction with teams can lead to everything from higher turnover to loss of productivity. If leaders are not present—if they are not empathetic and involved—how can they ever expect to make the sorts of personal connections that will inspire and motivate others to follow them?

One recommendation I have always made to leaders I coach is that they seek out the worst or least-desired job in their organization and then go spend quality time with the people who do it every day. I encourage leaders to spend time with the people who are hanging on to the lowest rung of the company ladder and to have them teach the leader about their job. Leaders soon find out what it takes to repair the weapons or ready the helicopter for flight status. Sometimes they even actually *remember* what it was like when they themselves once did that job; when they were stuck toiling in the trenches. They see for themselves how vital this seemingly menial task is to the overall success of the organization. And also how important the person is who is doing it.

Don't ride the back bench. Lead by example. Lead from the front.

THE PELICAN
AND THE FROG

THERE'S A TERRIFIC CARTOON that speaks volumes about the tenacity required for success. It's one of my all-time favorites and, appropriately enough, showcases a bullfrog as the hero.

In the Navy, the "Bull Frog" epithet recognizes the UDT/SEAL operator with the greatest amount of cumulative service following completion of Underwater Demolition Team Replacement Accession (UDTRA) or Basic Underwater Demolition/SEAL (BUD/S) training, regardless of rank.

According to Naval Special Warfare Command legend, "the Navy's connotation of the species comes from the days when UDT swimmers were glorified in song and movies as 'frogmen.'" The team boss was the Bull Frog. The name stuck and eventually was adopted by official order from Rear Admiral Richard Lyon, the first Bull Frog, who retired in 1981.

The UDT-SEAL Association began the tradition of sponsoring and awarding a trophy to the coveted Bull Frog. And in 2007, Rear Admiral Joseph D. Kernan made the award official by means of U.S. Navy instruction.

The Bull Frogs have been enlisted men, warrant officers, and commissioned officers. Even one of my SEAL heroes, the retired four-star admiral Eric T. Olson, once held the title. You can understand why I have a special affinity for amphibians.

And the poster?

Perhaps you've seen what's commonly called the "Never Give Up" poster. If not, it looks something like this: A tall white crane is standing on some placid shoreline surrounded by water lilies and lily pads. The bird has just plucked a fat, feisty frog from the pond bank and is struggling mightily to swallow the frog headfirst. Unfortunately for the crane, the frog—with half his body already down the bird's gullet—has clamped both of its "hands" around the crane's neck and is choking the bird with a death grip. The crane's eyes are bulging in astonishment and terror. The frog refuses to go down quietly. It's resolved to force a stalemate at the very least. I like to think the crane will soon cough up the tough toad.

The caption on the poster: "Never Give Up."

To me, this is what not-quitting looks like. It's about hope and determination.

It reminds me of a speech Winston Churchill gave to his alma mater, Harrow School, in 1941.

Never give in, never give in, never, never, never—in nothing, great or small, large or petty—never give in except to convictions of honor and good sense. Never yield to force; never yield to the apparently overwhelming might of the enemy. We stood all alone a year ago, and to many countries it seemed that our account was closed, we were finished. All this tradition of ours, our songs, our School history, this part of the history of this country, were gone and finished and liquidated.

Very different is the mood today. Britain, other nations thought, had drawn a sponge across her slate. But instead our country stood in the gap. There was no flinching and no thought of giving in; and by what seemed almost a miracle to those outside these Islands, though we ourselves never doubted it, we now find ourselves in a position where I say that we can be sure that we have only to persevere to conquer.

You never know how close you are to victory or success. Don't quit!

MENTORSHIP IS
MANDATORY

T RAINING YOUR REPLACEMENTS is a moral obligation for a
SEAL team. It's also good business. There is no finer leadership
trait than the willingness to develop the next generation's leaders. A
SEAL's personal example, experience, talents, and integrity go a long
way to achieving that.

In the military, seasoned senior enlisted men help train and groom
junior officers and teach them about life in the Navy; officers help junior enlisted sailors learn about life in general. And so on throughout
the chain of command. I'm convinced that in that sort of culture,
mentorship programs flourish. I was proud to be a "Sea Daddy" to
younger sailors and junior officers and have always prided myself on
mentoring others.

Great mentors always encourage successful protégés. I've always enjoyed giving people advice on how they can achieve their
goals, whether as SEALs or as business leaders trying to form high-
performing teams. At the same time, I actively always try to have a
mentor for myself, too. As an entrepreneur, I've benefited tremendously from the terrific wisdom and advice given to me by some of
my most successful clients. They are an inspiration to me. My mom,
too, was one of the very best mentors I've ever had!

Hard work has always been the most important element of my success. That said, I've had lots of help along the way. And because I am so excited and animated about what I do—my passion clearly shows through—people have always been willing to support me as a mentor. I am eternally grateful and do my best to share the things I've learned with others.

One of the last jobs I had in the Navy was being a mentor to kids who hoped to become SEALs. I helped these young kids navigate the Navy SEAL ascension process, and its specific requirements. I motivated them by example, and I know I made a difference in many of their lives just by giving them my time and attention. That was especially true for the African-American kids. As a black man, I felt a special kinship to these hard chargers and it was my distinct honor and special privilege to be their mentor.

As I've worked with the Young Presidents' Organization, I've witnessed firsthand how valuable it is for leaders to have the support of a network of fellow entrepreneurs and experienced executives to help grow a business. Like the young SEALs I mentor, these executives have taught me to learn from their successes as well as their mistakes.

Having a mentor whom you respect and who is willing to give you their time and attention is as valuable as an MBA in my estimation. Don't be shy about seeking one out. You should also give freely of yourself to someone you respect and in whom you really believe. Someone that you want to see succeed. Like me, you should consider mentoring—in both directions—as mandatory leader behavior.

LIONS LED BY
DONKEYS

DISMISSED BY SOME historians as a misleading caricature, the phrase "lions led by donkeys" is a term that's been used to describe the brave fighting men of the British infantry (the lions) during World War I and the incompetent—some even say indifferent—senior officers who sent them to slaughter (the donkeys).

According to a 1961 book by Alan Clark called *The Donkeys,* the phrase was attributed to a conversation between German generals Erich Ludendorff and Max Hoffmann:

LUDENDORFF: *The English soldiers fight like lions.*

HOFFMANN: *True. But don't we know that they are lions led by donkeys.*

While the veracity of the claim of incompetent British leadership in general and the quote itself specifically remain subject to hot historical debate, the leadership principle is clear: you've got to have the right people in the right positions if you hope to have success.

SEALs are lions, without question. Thankfully, we're also led by lions, not by donkeys or sheep from the disbursing office or supply store. It simply would not work if that were the case. For a team to be successful, not only do you have to have the right people on the bus—to use a popular business phrase—but those people have to be assigned to the proper seats as well.

Far too often I've seen chief executive officers make key personnel assignments with little or no regard to the critical team dynamics that will surely result. At one company I was counseling, the head of the sales force was a recently appointed, number-crunching accountant who was personal friends with the CEO. The boss implicitly trusted and valued the loyalty of the accountant. They had a terrific personal relationship and the CEO's trust and confidence was understandable. So when things started to go south in sales after a longtime director was fired for corruption, the CEO turned to his trusted lieutenant to help right the ship.

Not surprisingly, the accountant began to flounder in his new position. He couldn't have been more different in style and sensibility from the meat eaters he was now tasked with leading, coaching, and mentoring. While he understood and appreciated the CEO's sales goals like no one else, he lacked many of the competencies and personality traits that were essential to building and managing a fast-paced sales force. For example, he didn't know how to recruit salespeople—the sorts of lions required for this difficult kind of work. He had trouble managing gregarious, confident, Type A individuals, whether they were poor performers or sales stars. He was a painfully shy introvert, by nature, who had trouble coaching and inspiring his team. It was obvious to me after talking to the sales team that they didn't think he had much to teach them anyway. And they were right. Unfortunately, they needed to be taught new and innovative ways to seal their deals. They needed to be encouraged—incentivized—to crack cold clients and create new categories. But the accountant was simply not the guy for the gig. When he focused painfully on details during sales meetings, the sales team sat hungry for some big-picture opportunities and per-spectives that they felt were required for future success. Needless to say, the team continued to underperform and individuals were frustrated.

The accounting department suffered, too. They had lost a great manager and an asset who understood their mission and was pas-sionate about the numbers process.

It's clear how vital it is to pair the right people with the right posi-tions. The successful leader must skillfully recognize talent, develop it, and properly deploy it. Fortunately, the CEO listened to my advice and reversed his decision. He promoted one of the top members of the sales team to the job, showing faith in his team and a better under-standing of their culture. The newly motivated sales manager took to the job and quickly turned things around. It turned out he had bright strategies and tactics that the previous boss had disregarded but were spot-on for mission success.

Returning the accountant to his rightful place was a more deli-cate matter. It was essential that the move not be seen as a failure on the accountant's part. Thankfully, the CEO tied the return to a promotion—he made him an assistant vice president of the company, with even more financial oversight and responsibility. It also included a role as counselor to the CEO. Without question, the accountant was deserving of a greater role and prominence within the company—it just wasn't on the sales team. In the end, both the accountant and the new sales director blossomed in their new roles. The CEO benefited from new ideas, urgency, and energy on the sales floor and a more cohesive sales team. His new vice president continued to faithfully serve him and the company in new and innovative ways. In the end, much to the company's benefit, by ensuring the right people were in the right places, the CEO began unleashing the inner lions of many other employees.

I can't think of anything more trying for a leader than the responsibility to put the right person in the right place. Or anything quite as essential. You've got to get the people right. As an Arab proverb would have it, "An army of sheep led by a lion would defeat an army of lions led by a sheep." Hooyah.

COMPETENCE AND
CHARACTER

NAVY SEALS are enormously motivated by three things: honor, courage, and commitment.

The naysayers out there may scoff at such a notion but I'm here to tell you that it's a very real driving force to my fraternity of pipe-swinging frogmen. We believe in truth, justice, and the American way. We salute when we hear the national anthem. We want to risk our lives to defend the weak and defenseless or, put another way, to beat down bullies who prey on the unsuspecting. Those are some of our values.

Values are nothing to be scoffed at, whether on Wall Street or in Waziristan. They are a big part of what propels Navy SEALs to volunteer for a life of danger—that and a guarantee of adventure and an uncommon life. Your own corporate and personal values as a leader will be much of what motivates and drives your employees.

When I think of my teammates, two words come to mind: *competence* and *character*. They are born out of the shared values that we hold. Because SEALs are filled with copious amounts of each, they are able to inspire trust, a necessary ingredient for any successful leader. As the late bestselling author Stephen Covey describes it, character includes your integrity, motive, and intent with people.

Competence includes your capabilities, skills, results, and track record. Both dimensions are vital, Covey contends. I could not agree more. I trusted my teammates with my very life for more than two decades because I trusted their competence as operators and their character as individuals. I knew their values. Rarely was I ever let down.

The late General H. "Stormin' Norman" Schwarzkopf, my supreme commander during Operation Desert Storm in the early 1990s, said that character and competence were essential to being a twenty-first-century leader.

In an address at West Point to the Army's future leaders, Schwarzkopf said that he had met a lot of leaders who were highly competent but were only in it for themselves. They didn't have character. "For every job they did well in the Army, they sought reward in the form of promotions, in the form of awards and decorations, in the form of getting ahead at the expense of somebody else, in the form of another piece of paper that awarded them another degree," he said. "The only reason why they wanted that was because it was a sure road to faster promotion, to somehow get to the top. You see, these were very competent people, but they lacked character. . . ."

Schwarzkopf went on. "I've seen competent leaders who stood in front of a platoon and saw it as a platoon. But I've seen great leaders who stood in front of a platoon and saw it as 44 individuals, each of whom had his hopes, each of whom had his aspirations, each of whom wanted to live, each of whom wanted to do good. So, you must have character. To lead in the 21st Century, to take soldiers, sailors, airmen, marines, coastguardsmen into battle, you will be required to have both competence and character."

In the business of winning wars and deterring aggression, competence will always be the more important of the two traits. You can't have a SEAL team leader with impeccable character who can't fight his way out of a wet paper bag. That's just the reality of the responsibilities of our fighting forces. But character has and always will continue to count for a great deal.

I always ask my business friends if their company clearly values respect and promotes character and competence. I ask whether their corporate training and development programs—if they even have them—offer ways for their employees to improve both things. Does the culture value character in the messages it sends, the products it delivers, and the decisions that affect the lives and careers of the employees who work there? Does competence trump character at all costs or not? Do the pay, benefits, and advancement systems recognize the values of character and competence and reward the same? Are issues of questionable or poor character ever overlooked in favor of the bottom line?

Competence and character are a remarkable duo. Customers know it. The remarkable leader does, too.

GET A SWIM BUDDY

W E ALL NEED PEOPLE we can trust in this life. People we can count on to check our six (SEAL-speak for what's behind us), to tell us the truth or to give us a reality check when we make—or are about to make—a very stupid fashion or financial decision.

In the SEALs, we have what are known as Swim Buddies. It starts in BUD/S when the instructors pair us up with another sailor for what the Navy likes to call two-man integrity. The Swim Buddy concept is a microcosm of what teamwork is all about. It's teamwork at the prime level. Everywhere you go, you take a Swim Buddy with you: To the head, to the chow hall, to the pit of punishment. It's all done together. Team first.

A Swim Buddy is a support system, not unlike a police officer's partner. Swim Buddies hold each other accountable and are responsible for each other, too. If you get into trouble, it's your Swim Buddy who will most likely be the first to try to get you out of it, and vice versa. Swim Buddies are not necessarily friends, but most definitely partners. Because we know that no man is an island, we don't do anything without them.

I emphasize the Swim Buddy concept in my seminars because it is that basic building block of teamwork. Do you have anything of the sort at your organization?

One company I worked with took hard hold of the idea and incorporated it into their new employee orientation program. For the first year of a new person's employment, this company paired the new guy with a veteran coworker from the same department. For several months, the two were tied at the hip. They attended new employee orientation meetings together, company functions, and certain training programs. As the company has it set up, the veteran attends a certain percentage of every training program the new guy attends and they have a certain number of scheduled luncheons and coffee breaks together each month and attend personal development meetings together, too. Company officials tell me that what began as a simple way to make the new employee orientation program more meaningful has turned into team building at its finest. The new employee is never lost in the corporate shuffle or forced to navigate alone. At the same time, the veteran employee gets fresh perspectives on ideas and issues that can be more quickly relayed to management.

Wouldn't it be great if every employee had a Swim Buddy that he or she could turn to when they needed a helping hand or second set of eyes? A buddy whom they could, say, bounce a presentation off of before they have to deliver it to management? To create effective teams, you've got to create effective teammates first.

That notion extends outside the corporate walls and into the larger business culture as well. One of my best Swim Buddies is Yacov Wrocherinsky, founder and CEO of Infinity Info Systems, a New York City–based information technology consulting firm focused on customer relationship management (CRM) and business analytics solutions for clients in the financial, life sciences, business services, media, and manufacturing/distribution industries around the world.

Yacov has been both a mentor and friend to me for years. We met when he attended my first Leadership Under Fire event for the Young Presidents' Organization.

Yacov, in turn, relies on trusted corporate partners to be his Swim Buddies when a business problem or opportunity presents itself.

Infinity is based in the United States but its customers are global. Yacov and his teams find tech solutions for companies in as many as eighty different countries. To that end, he aggressively establishes relationships with companies like his and creates global alliances with like-minded colleagues who are, in turn, better positioned to provide the local service.

"Everybody is not your enemy," Yacov says. "You will be amazed by the energy you can draw from other people. You can grow and find new opportunities from other people, other resources. Some of my competitors often serve as my collaborative partners!

"My new partners—my Swim Buddies—provide the local expertise and service but they are armed with Infinity technologies," he said. "It's a mutually beneficial relationship that provides the best value to the customer. My partners and I are not competitors but colleagues.

"There are people out there who are as good or better than I am at what I do, and I can learn something from them," he said. "If they can provide a better service to my customer at the national, state, or hyperlocal environment, why wouldn't I take advantage of that?"

Who is your Swim Buddy?

TAKE CARE OF YOURSELF

O N ANY GIVEN DAY, a leader is easily consumed by his or her commitment to contemplate, assess, and address issues directly affecting the business and the people they lead. Countless hours of every day are consumed with solving problems or anticipating outcomes. The servant leader struggles to continually empower his people, cares about their well-being, and ensures they are trained and equipped for any mission they may face.

But who looks out for the leader? Sadly, too often the answer is no one. Or very few of them, I should say, outside of your very best friends or family. But as I've grown older and more senior in my various leadership roles, I've learned that in order for me to be the best, most attentive leader I can be, it is imperative that I prioritize my own health and well-being now and again in order to best take care of my people.

As a SEAL, that was relatively easy to do. I mean, physical fitness is ingrained in the corporate culture. Everywhere you turned there was a pull-up bar to mount, a stack of weights to attack, or an obstacle course to swarm. The opportunity for fitness was always there, as long as one had the commitment.

And given the competitive nature of all SEALs, a commitment to fitness and wellness was never hard to come by. SEALs are expected to always lead by example. When I was a chief, for example, it was a matter of personal pride for me to be able to run farther and faster, swim longer and deeper, and push harder and smarter than the younger petty officers who looked up to me. In order to drive my team forward and to inspire my men along the way, I had to be in the best physical and mental shape possible. Of course, I personally benefited from the commitment, too.

So, starting today, make a commitment to take better care of one more essential employee: yourself. Do for yourself what you consistently do for others. Create opportunities for and cultures of fitness that will help steel your spine for the challenges you know lie ahead.

As a parent, I often have to work hard to carve out time in my chaotic schedule to spend with my son and daughter. You must do the very same thing with your fitness regime.

Tina, a bank CEO in upstate New York, relished the physical training we gave her at LUF and began infusing it into her daily life. The physical and mental benefits were amazing, she said.

"My new physical stamina directly affects my mental stamina," she said. "I have more bandwidth to attack problems and issues. I can also process complex problems much more clearly."

Tina also believes that working out provides her more precious "white space" during the day to sort through things and be open to new opportunities.

"For example, I can replay conversations I've had with my clients in my head when I'm working out. I can noodle them with more time and clarity. I can also chose to listen to a book on tape and be enlightened by the ideas and accomplishments of others."

When you maintain a regular commitment to personal fitness (both mental and physical)—and I'm talking about just thirty minutes a day, three or four times a week—you'll have more energy and stamina to tackle life's daily challenges. You'll be more focused, confident, and creative, more able to stave off the effects of depression, and perhaps even to delay the debilitating effects of certain diseases. You'll think more clearly, I guarantee. An added benefit: you'll continue to be an inspiration to others, long after the workday is over.

DROWNPROOF
YOUR BUSINESS

ONE OF THE TOUGHEST PIECES of Navy SEAL training is known as drownproofing. In this pool exercise, SEAL candidates must learn to swim—to survive, really—with both their hands and feet bound together. Drownproofing was developed by a swimming coach named Fred Lanoue, and adopted by the Navy and the SEALs as part of our standard training.

The idea behind Lanoue's technique is that a person can survive a water disaster without sinking or drowning, even if they are hurt or disabled. Lanoue posited that most people are "floaters" when their lungs are filled with air. All that is needed for survival is to remain calm in the water and to pop their head above the water now and again for a lifesaving gulp of air. And then they return to the float position.

To successfully master the technique, SEALs jump into a nine-foot-deep pool with their feet together at the ankles and their arms bound behind their back. They calmly remain in a near vertical position with just the top of their heads poking out of the water. Several times each minute, the SEAL will use his arms and legs to create just enough downward pressure so that their head can break the surface just long enough to snatch a deep breath of fresh air, enough to fill up their lungs, and then revert back into the relaxed vertical float. To pass the test, SEALS must bob, float, swim, and do some backward flips in a set amount of time.

It sounds terrifying, but it's relatively easy to learn and most people are quick to master the technique. I'm not a tall guy, but I am pretty big. And even big guys like me had little trouble with drownproofing.

Learning this technique was an incredible confidence booster for me. While it's an insurance policy at the most basic level, it's also a way to ensure SEALs overcome any fear of being stranded in the ocean. Once I knew I could survive for hours in any water evolution—even if I was badly injured or near incapacitated—I was more confident in my other water training. That confidence helped me vastly improve other important skills.

Business leaders should look to develop similar "drownproofing" training centered on a business-specific catastrophe they could some-day face. It may not be a water obstacle you'll face. It could be a power outage or a lack of secure communications.

How can you drownproof your organization and employees to face the crisis? What's your drownproofing event?

REPUTATION IS
EVERYTHING

WARREN BUFFETT once famously said, "It takes twenty years to build a reputation and five minutes to ruin it. If you think about that, you'll do things differently."

The wise leader, like Buffett, knows that reputations matter. The relationships you are able to build, the revenues you will generate, and the loyalty of employees and customers alike are all dependent on your personal brand—your reputation. It determines your value position, based on how well people trust and respect you. The expectations they have of you. A good reputation greases the skids and opens the door. A bad one can derail options and block pathways.

Whether online or off, your personal and professional reputation is something that sticks, and must be guarded and protected at all costs.

For SEALs, reputations are built at BUD/S. And it's amazing how fast they develop and quickly—and how far—they spread. When a candidate is labeled as someone who continually makes excuses, is always unprepared, or who can't control their temper, for example, that reputation will precede them everywhere they go. At BUD/S we remind SEALs every day that their reputation begins *now*.

A smart leader sweats the small stuff. Do what's expected of you and do it to the best of your ability.

ATTENTION TO DETAIL

I N MY BUSINESS, 360-degree security is not 359 degrees. With the latter, there's a hole in my defenses—tiny as it might be—where a bad guy can penetrate. For SEALs, such attention to detail is a life-or-death distinction.

For business leaders, attention to detail is often the difference between something good and something amazingly great. That concept was captured in a terrific little story I read back in 2011, just after the death of Apple CEO Steve Jobs.

The story, a blog post really, was penned by Vic Gundotra, the executive behind Google+, the company's social media platform. Gundotra wrote about a phone call he had with Jobs on Sunday morning. Jobs had called Gundotra when he was in church and Gundotra hadn't picked up the phone. The return call went something like this:

> "Hey Steve—this is Vic," I said. "I'm sorry I didn't answer your call earlier. I was in religious services, and the caller ID said unknown, so I didn't pick up."
>
> Steve laughed. He said, "Vic, unless the caller ID said 'GOD,' you should never pick up during services."
>
> I laughed nervously. After all, while it was customary for Steve to call during the week upset about something, it was unusual for

him to call me on Sunday and ask me to call his home. I wondered what was so important?

"So Vic, we have an urgent issue, one that I need addressed right away. I've already assigned someone from my team to help you, and I hope you can fix this tomorrow," said Steve.

"I've been looking at the Google logo on the iPhone and I'm not happy with the icon. The second 'o' in Google doesn't have the right yellow gradient. It's just wrong and I'm going to have Greg fix it tomorrow. Is that okay with you?"

In the end, when I think about leadership, passion, and attention to detail, I think back to the call I received from Steve Jobs on a Sunday morning in January. It was a lesson I'll never forget. CEOs should care about details. Even shades of yellow. On a Sunday.

Pay attention. It matters.

ACKNOWLEDGMENTS

I would like to give my sincerest thanks to Lance O'Connor for his continued guidance and friendship. At times we haven't always seen eye to eye, but Lance, you have always been a constant beacon to me in my quest for success. No matter how reluctant I have been at times to take your advice, you always managed to bring out the best in me. You constantly challenge me to raise the bar each and every time, and inspire me to be a better leader than I was the day before. For all that you do, and for your unwavering support, I am eternally grateful. You taught me, "It is not what *they* think of you, it is what *you* think of you."

Next, I would like to give special thanks to Danya, Liz, and Shelva. Without your professionalism, support, and guidance, I would not be where I am today. You bring a unique passion and quality to everything that you are a part of. What I have learned from you three has made me a better leader, listener, and, most of all, person. Thank you.

Special thanks to Chris Lawson, my friend and cowriter, and his family, for the hours, weeks, and months spent putting the words to the page. You are in my heart, and in the front of my mind. My friend, we create what we want, and choice is the first step in being successful. Thank you for agreeing to do something special. You are an inspiration.

I would like to express my deepest gratitude to a man who has given me some of the most valuable advice and guidance in my professional and personal life: Yacov Wrocherinsky. Yacov, you are a man who embodies the words he speaks, a man who practices the lessons he gives. Your support over the years has meant the world to me, and the wisdom you've imparted will have a lasting impact on my life. You've shown me that even the toughest businessman can have a soft heart. What you do for others before yourself is a testament to the rare and genuine soul I know you to be. Thank you for showing me this.

Last, but not least, I would like to thank my wife. You are the foundation that makes my success possible. Your faith in me has never wavered, and your support is what keeps me going. You have been a constant source of love, and together we've built a life that I cherish. I thank you for our two beautiful children and the love you give me every day that warms my heart. I feel truly blessed to have you in my life—words will never express that enough. Simply put, I want to say, "Thank you."

And to America—I feel extraordinarily blessed to have had the opportunity to serve and be a part of the greatest country on earth. I believe she offers enormous opportunities to each and every one of us—we just have to be willing to work hard and reach for them. Remember: "*There is never a traffic jam on the extra mile.*"

—Rob Roy

Special thanks to Rob Roy for the opportunity to do something special. You are a friend and an inspiration. To the motivated cadre of SOT-G—especially Wolly, Geoff, Jeff, and Pops—thanks for putting up with a reporter's endless questions and observations. You motivate the heck out of me. Thanks also goes to Yacov Wrocherinsky for the pep talks, context, and camaraderie, especially that ill-fated and unintended slink down into old Mexico!

Thanks, too, to our agent, Zach Schisgal, who got us to the dance.

Thanks for the confidence and determination, Z. To Roger Scholl, our editor at Random House, thank you for the wisdom, encouragement, and endless great ideas. I could not have asked for a better mentor. To my wife, Jessica, and our sons Max, Ben, and Cam, thank you all for putting up with a year of "I've got to go work on the book" excuses from me. Your wonderful support and patience helped make a dream of mine come true.

Last, thank you to the men and women of the United States military, whose character, competence, and selfless service never cease to amaze me. The same goes for the hard-working and tireless businessmen and women who fuel this great economy of ours. Leaders, all.

—Chris Lawson